Government Today

by Beverly Vaillancourt

New Readers Press ● Syracuse, New York

cover photo:
National Geographic Society photographer
courtesy U.S. Capitol Historical Society

ISBN 0-88336-856-0

© 1985

New Readers Press

Publishing Division of Laubach Literacy International

Box 131, Syracuse, New York 13210

EACH ONE TEACH ONE

Printed in the United States of America

Designed by Sally Rubadeau

9   8   7   6   5   4   3

Foreword

This book is about government. Our government. In it you will learn how the government works and how it affects you.

Government is large and there are many layers to it. It wasn't always as large as it is now. Times have changed since the first Americans wrote the plan for our government. Today, government has a lot more jobs to do. It has more services to provide. And there are more people to do these services for.

When we think about our government we usually think of Washington, D.C., our nation's capitol. This is where the president lives. Washington is also where our country's lawmakers meet. But states also have governments and state capitols. There are local governments, too.

Government is all around you. And you know what? You're a special part of government. In our country, power comes from the people. People use their power when they vote.

Government affects your daily life. Laws are made for people to obey. At the same time, people can work to change the laws. You really can be a part of government.

The most important thing any citizen can do is learn more about government. This book is going to help you do just that.

Table of Contents

America's Beginnings

How we became the United States of America is a long story. At first, we were just a group of colonies. We belonged to England. The colonies were very different from each other. The colonies did not work well together, either. There was very little about the first colonies that was united.

The colonies were forced to unite when they went to war against England. This was called the Revolutionary War. The colonies won their freedom in this war. After the Revolutionary War, the colonies needed to write a plan of government. They wrote the Constitution.

How did the colonies become their own country? What does the Constitution say? You will learn the answers to these questions in this unit.

By the end of this unit you should be able to:

● explain what the Constitution is.
● explain how the national and state governments work together.
● explain the three branches of government.

1. We Are a Democracy

> **Words to know**
>
> democracy   colonies
> colonists

Government makes the laws for us. Every country needs some form of government. There are many kinds of government in the world today. Our form of government is called a **democracy.**

What is a democracy? In a democracy, people have a say in the making of laws. The power to make laws comes from the people.

Was America the first country to have a democracy? No, America was not the first country in the world to have a democracy. Democracies are not new. Athens, a city in ancient Greece, had one of the first democracies almost 2,500 years ago. In fact, the word *democracy* comes from two Greek words that mean "people rule."

Athens had what is called a direct democracy. That means that every adult man had the right to vote and play a part in government. (Women,

slaves, and men under 20, however, were not allowed to vote.)

Do we have a direct democracy? No, we do not have a direct democracy. Ours is called a representative democracy. That means that we elect the people who make the laws.

Compared to the United States, Athens was very small. Over 200 million people live in our country today. There is no way that every adult person could vote on every decision that government needs to make. It would take too long. Nothing would get done.

In a representative democracy people are elected to make decisions for the whole country. If the country is unhappy with the people elected, they can be replaced. In the next election, new people would be voted for.

Have we always been a democracy? No, we have not always been a democracy. In fact, for a long time we weren't even our own country.

Our country is made of people from all over the world. The first people to live here were the Indians. In 1492, Christopher Columbus sailed from Spain to America. Others began sailing to America. Many claimed land for their home countries.

Soon many people came to settle in America. They came for different reasons. Some came looking for riches. Some wanted to make a better life in a new land. Others came so that they could be free to go to the church of their choice.

Many people came from England to live in America. They built towns. This settled land was divided into **colonies.** The people who lived in the colonies were called **colonists**. There were 13 English colonies. The colonists in these colonies had to obey England's laws. England was ruled by King George III.

The colonists began to dislike England making laws for them. They wanted to make their own laws. They did not like having to pay taxes to England. The colonists were becoming very angry with England.

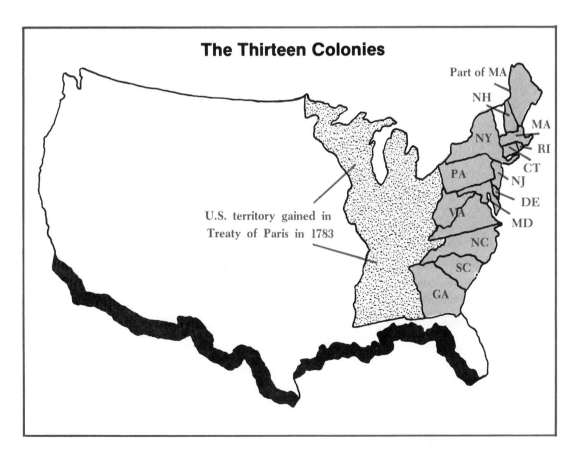

The Thirteen Colonies

Part of MA
NH
MA
NY
RI
CT
PA
NJ
DE
VA
MD
NC
SC
GA

U.S. territory gained in Treaty of Paris in 1783

2. The Colonies Revolt

In 1774, men chosen from each of the colonies met in Philadelphia. They were called the First Continental Congress. They met to discuss the problems they were having with England.

What did they decide to do? The First Continental Congress decided to write a letter to King George III of England. The letter asked the King to respect the rights of the colonists. The colonists did not ask to be free from England. In 1774, few men wanted to break away from England and begin their own country.

What happened to change their minds? Things between the colonies and England became worse. They could not agree on anything. King George did not like the letter the colonists had sent him. England decided that she had a right to rule the colonies. The colonies decided that they wanted to be **independent**—free from England. The first shot of the Revolutionary War was fired in 1775.

After the Revolutionary War began, the colonists decided to write a **document** (a written statement). This document would explain to England and the rest of the world why the colonists had a right to be free. They called this document the Declaration of Independence.

Who wrote the Declaration of Independence? A group of men were given the job of writing the Declaration of Independence. Thomas Jefferson was in charge of this group.

The Declaration was an important document. It told the world (and King George) that:

- all men are created equal.
- all men have certain rights.
- governments are created to protect these rights.
- governments get their power from the people.
- when government fails to protect the rights of the people, it is the people's duty to overthrow it.

Everyone who helped write the Declaration signed it.

Did the Declaration of Independence give the colonists their freedom? No, the Declaration did not give Americans their freedom. They had to win their freedom by fighting a war. The Revolutionary War was hard on the colonists.

They were not ready for war. They had little food stored. They had poor clothing. Their guns were old. They had no training in how to fight a war.

England's army was well-trained. She had one of the best armies and navies in the world. English soldiers had many supplies. They had good guns, too.

Why didn't England win the war? There are several reasons why England did not win the Revolutionary War.

Americans knew they had to fight hard. Many died. This made them want to win even more. George Washington was the leader of our army. He told them not to give in.

England fought hard, too. But England was also fighting wars with Spain and France. It became hard for England to fight so many wars at once.

Then France decided to help the colonies. With her help, they were finally able to defeat the English. At last, the Revolutionary War was over. It had lasted longer than anyone thought it would. It lasted six years.

They were now free to begin a new government. They became the United States of America. But as they soon learned, it was not easy to begin a new country.

National Archives

This famous painting by John Trumbull shows the signing of the Declaration of Independence. Fifty-six men signed the Declaration.

3. The Articles of Confederation

Once the colonies had become the United States, they found themselves in need of a plan of government. We call a written plan of government a **constitution.** Our first plan of government was called the **Articles of Confederation.**

What were the Articles of Confederation? The Articles of Confederation were our first try at self-government. Some call it our first constitution.

The Articles of Confederation didn't work very well. It was too weak. The Articles of Confederation did not give the national government enough power. The states were afraid of a strong national (federal) government. They wanted the states to have most of the power.

There were several reasons for this. One, the early states were not like the states today. Today we think of ourselves as Americans. In 1781, when the Articles of Confederation were written, people thought of themselves as New Yorkers or Rhode Islanders.

The states had very little in common. The war had united them, but they still didn't trust each other very much.

Second, the states remembered only too well their bad experience with King George. They thought that if they had a strong central government, it might abuse its power. This is also why the Articles of Confederation did not call for a president. (There was a president of the Congress, but he was not like the president we have today.) The states

In 1787 the Constitutional Convention met to write a new plan of government. It was clear that the Articles of Confederation were not working.

thought a president might become too much like a king.

For example, Congress could declare war. In fact, it was fighting a war—the Revolutionary War. But Congress could not raise an army. It had to ask the states to supply men.

How did the government run under the Articles of Confederation? Under the Articles of Confederation there was a Congress. Congress had some powers including the power to make war. But it had little power to enforce laws.

And Congress could not make taxes. If it needed money it had to ask the states for it. The states could always refuse.

As you can see, this made it very hard to run a country. It also made it hard to run a war.

Under the Articles of Confederation, the states had the most power. Each state had an equal vote in Congress. But the states were not happy. When the Revolutionary War was over, there was little to unite the states. The states fought with each other. Finally, the states decided it was time for a change.

4. The Constitution

The states sent men to a **convention** (large meeting) in Philadelphia in 1787. The convention's job was to write a new constitution. The convention was called the Constitutional Convention. The states argued about many things at the convention.

What was one of the arguments at the convention? One argument was over how much power the federal government should have. The states knew that if they were going to be a country, then power had to be shared among a federal government and state governments. This idea of sharing power is called **federalism.** The question was, how much power should the national government have and how much should the states have?

What was another argument? Another argument at the convention was, how should the states be represented in the federal government. The large and small states were very bitter on this issue. Each was afraid to lose control to the other.

Under the Articles of Confederation each state had one vote in the Congress. The small states wanted it to stay this way. The big states argued that they should have more votes in Congress because they had more people. The small states said this was unfair.

How were these arguments settled? It took a long time. Each side fought hard. Sometimes it looked as if they would never agree. But finally, the states decided to **compromise.** That is, each side decided to give a little in order to get a little.

The states were able to write a constitution once they compromised. The Constitution they wrote is the same one we have today.

The Constitution of the United States is divided into parts. The first part is called the Preamble. The Preamble says that the Constitution was written so that the country could be more united. The Constitution was written so that the country would be well protected and the people safe. And, most importantly, it was written to protect the rights of people. In writing the Constitution, the states joined together to form a government for all the people.

The second part of the Constitution is called the Articles. There are seven articles. Each one is divided into sections. Each article tells about a different power of the government.

The Constitution even gives a way for it to be changed. An **amendment** is needed to change the Constitution. An amendment is simply a written change that is added to the Constitution. It becomes a part of the Constitution. Today, there are 26 amendments to the Constitution.

The amendments form the last part of the Constitution. These amendments talk about the rights of the people. The first ten amendments are called the Bill of Rights. The Bill of Rights was added to the Constitution in 1791.

What does the Constitution say? The Constitution says many things. It is the framework for our entire system of government. It says:

- that we will have a representational democracy.
- that power will be shared among the national and state governments (federalism).
- that there will be a separation of powers.

How does federalism work? The Constitution created a federal system of government. This means that the federal government and the state governments have to work together.

The states were afraid of a strong federal government. Yet, they had learned that the central government they had under the Articles of Confederation was not strong enough.

What the Constitution finally decided was that certain powers would be given to the federal government. Some powers would be given to the state governments. Other powers would belong to both.

After the Constitution was written, arguments over how much power the states should have continued. They continued until the Civil War. The states in the south claimed they had the right to leave the Union and begin their own country. The North said they couldn't and the Civil War began.

Of course, the southern states were not allowed to leave the Union. The Civil War decided once and for all that the national government was supreme. That is, the federal government has the last word when it comes to matters involving the whole country.

5. The Separation of Powers

Words to know	
executive	judicial
legislative	checks and balances
enforce	interpret

The writers of the Constitution felt it was not enough to divide powers among the federal and state governments. They decided that the power to govern had to be divided up even more. They decided that there should be three branches of government.

What is one branch of government? One branch of government is the **executive.** The executive branch is made up of the president, the vice-president, and other people who help the president. The job of the executive branch is to **enforce** (carry out) the laws of the country.

What is another branch of government? The **legislative** branch is another branch of government. This branch makes the laws for the country. It is often referred to as Congress. Congress has two parts called houses. One house is called the Senate. The other is called the House of Representatives.

Remember the argument between the large and small states? The kind of Congress we have today is a direct result of this argument. The small states wanted each state to have one vote. The large states wanted each state to have a different number of votes depending on how many people lived in that state. The more people who lived in a state, the more votes that state would have.

The compromise the states agreed on was this. Congress would be divided into two houses. In one house, the Senate, each state would be represented equally. Each state would have two representatives called senators. This pleased the small states.

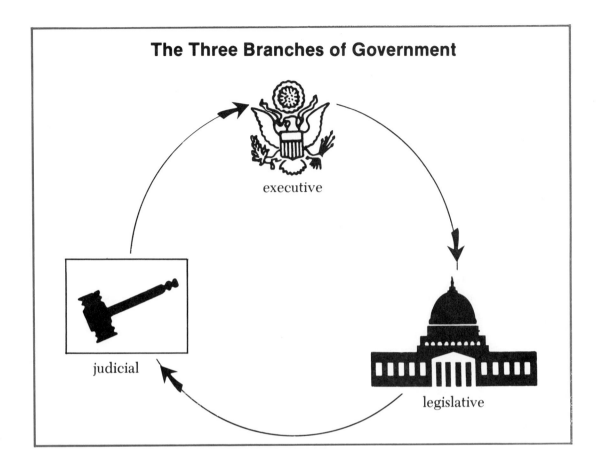

The Three Branches of Government

executive

judicial

legislative

In the House of Representatives, each state would have a different number of representatives. This number would be decided by the number of people who lived in the state. Thus, the states who had more people would have more votes. The large states were pleased with this. (The people who sit in the House of Representatives are simply called representatives.)

The houses work together to make laws. For something to become law, it must be passed by both houses.

What is the last branch of government? The last branch of government is the **judicial.** The judicial branch is made up of the country's courts. It is the job of the courts to **interpret** the laws. This means that the courts explain the laws. They decide when a law has been broken. One particular court, the Supreme Court, has the job of interpreting the Constitution.

How do the three branches work together? The Constitution gives each branch a job to do. But these jobs overlap. They were meant to. This is part of the **checks and balances** of our system. Each branch has ways of checking, or limiting, the powers of the other two. This way, no single branch of government can become too powerful.

Unit 1 Summary

Our country is made up of states. The states are united together under one government. We are the United States of America.

We were not always united. Before we became the United States, we were a group of colonies. The colonies belonged to England. The colonies grew tired of English rule. They decided to be free from England. The Revolutionary War was fought.

After the war was won, there was little to unite the colonies. In 1787, a convention met in Philadelphia. The purpose of this convention was to write a plan of government. They wrote the Constitution.

The Constitution is the highest law of the land. The laws we follow come from the Constitution. It is the framework for our entire system of government. Three important ideas in the Constitution are:

- that we will have a representational democracy.
- that power will be shared among the national and state governments.
- that there will be a separation of powers.

We have a representational democracy. This means that the people govern through representatives. The people decide who should speak in government for them. The people elect their representatives. This way the people have a say in the laws that are made for them.

The Constitution gave some powers to the federal government. Some powers were given to the state governments. Some powers were meant to be shared. This sharing of powers is called federalism.

The writers of the Constitution decided to further divide the powers of governments. They did this because they did not want any one person to be too powerful. They divided (or separated) the government into three branches. The three branches are: the executive, legislative, and judicial branches.

Each branch has a special job. The executive branch carries out the laws. The legislative branch writes the laws. The judicial branch interprets the laws. The three branches work together.

UNIT 2

The President and Vice-President

The president, vice-president, and other people who are part of the president's staff form the executive branch. The head of the executive branch is the president.

The president's role has grown in power since it was first designed by the writers of the Constitution. Many did not trust a strong president. They wanted to be sure that the nation would not be ruled by just one person. So when they wrote the Constitution they gave the president limited powers.

Over the years, the various presidents have changed the direction of the office. Today, the president is seen as the leader and spokesman for the country. Often, the beliefs and ideas of the president set the direction for the country.

Just how is the president elected? What are the jobs of the president? Why do these jobs hold so much power? What is the role of the vice-president? You will learn the answers to all these questions in this unit.

By the end of this unit, you should be able to:

- explain the steps in electing the president and vice-president.
- list the five jobs of the president.
- explain the role of the vice-president.

6. Who Can Be President?

Words to know

candidate   political party
campaigning

The election of the president and vice-president is a very important part of our government. Many people would like to become president of the United States.

Can anyone become president? A search must be made for the person who shows the most outstanding qualities. The Constitution has little to say about who can be president. It states only that a person must:

- be a citizen born in this country.
- be at least 35 years old.
- be a resident of the United States for 14 years.

If a person meets all of these requirements, then that person can run for president.

What kind of people have become president? Although someone must be at least 35 to run for president, most presidents have been at least 55. Also, most presidents have been married and well-known. Many presidents held important government jobs before being elected president. To date, all of our presidents have been white men. Probably, this will not always be true.

How does someone become president? It is difficult to be elected president. The election process is long and hard. Most people who wish to run for president will first have to win the support of their **political party**.

What is a political party? People who belong to a political party share the same ideas about government. Today, there are two major political parties in the United States. They are the Republicans and the Democrats.

How does someone win the support of their party? The first thing that a **candidate** (someone who wants to be elected) must do is let everyone know they are running. This can cost a lot of money. Candidates must do a lot of traveling. They visit cities and walk the streets shaking hands and even kissing babies. The candidates must give many speeches. And whenever possible

The 1984 presidential candidate, Walter Mondale, and his running mate, Geraldine Ferraro, make a campaign stop in New York City. Presidential and vice-presidential candidates travel across the U.S. to gain people's support.

they try to get on TV or radio. That way they know many people will be listening to them.

Candidates also need to attract people who are willing to work for them. Usually, these people belong to the same political party as the candidate. These people may hang posters or make phone calls to try and get their candidate elected. They will work together as a team. Most will not receive any money for their work. They do it because they believe the person they are working for would make the best president.

The speeches, the traveling, the hand shaking, and all the work done by the workers is part of the candidate's attempt to be elected. This is called **campaigning.** It begins as soon as a candidate decides to run for office.

7. Primary Elections

Words to know

primary	independents
delegates	nominate

Campaigning is a lot of work. Candidates will work hard to win as many **primary** elections as they can. Primaries are the first step in many kinds of elections. They give people a chance to show support for a candidate.

What do primary elections decide? Primary elections help decide who will run for office. All fifty states use primary elections to choose who will run in local, state, and federal elections.

How does the presidential primary work? Each party has a primary. Primaries are run by the states. Some states have a direct primary. Other states have an indirect primary.

Consolidated News Pictures from ISP

Delegates show their support for Geraldine Ferraro at the Democratic convention in San Francisco.

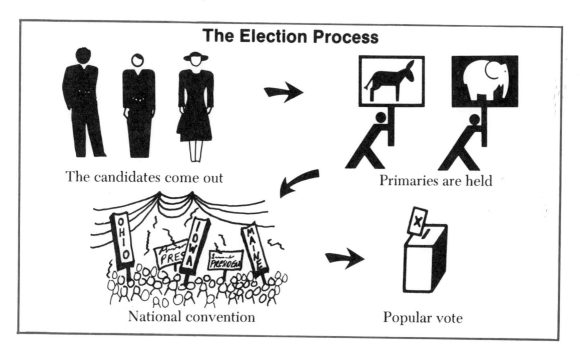

The Election Process

The candidates come out

Primaries are held

National convention

Popular vote

In the direct primary, all of a party's candidates will have their names placed on a state ballot. The people of the state then vote for the candidate of their choice.

In the indirect primary, people choose **delegates** to represent them. The delegates say they will support one of the candidates.

Does a person have to belong to a party to vote in a primary election? In some states a person must belong to a political party. Then that person can vote in his party's primary election. This is called a closed primary. For example, in a closed primary only Democrats could vote in the Democratic primary.

Do all states have closed primaries? No, some states have open primaries. All voters may vote in an open primary. It does not matter which party the

voter belongs to. Even **independents**, people who do not belong to a political party, may vote in open primaries.

What happens after the presidential primary? Each political party holds a national convention after the presidential primary. This is a meeting of all the delegates from each state. All the party's candidates are there.

The delegates **nominate**, or choose, from these candidates the person who will be the party's choice for president. They also choose a person to run for vice-president. The candidates who are nominated run as a team.

After their nomination, the party's candidates must still campaign. This time they want to win the support of all voters. They must do more traveling and make more speeches. Their workers will work long hours trying to get them elected. They will campaign up to the last minute on election day.

8. Election Day

Words to know	
electors	popular vote
electoral college	inauguration

There is a presidential election every four years in November. This is when the people vote. It is called a **popular vote.** As you will learn, this vote does not elect the president and the vice-president.

Do people vote directly for the president and vice-president? No, people do not vote directly for either the president or the vice-president. When people vote for someone to be president, they really vote for **electors.** Electors represent the people and vote for a president and vice-president.

How does this system of electors work? Each state has a group of electors. These electors are called the **electoral college.** The number of electors each state has is equal to the number of representatives it has in Congress.

Almost all of the time the electors vote for the same candidates that most people in their state voted for. In other words, the candidate who wins the popular vote receives all the electoral votes of that state.

When does the electoral college vote? Each state sets the date for when its electoral college will vote. It is after the popular vote in November. Usually, it is sometime in mid-December.

When do the new president and vice-president take office? The new president and vice-president take office on January 20. This event is called **Inauguration** Day.

A speech is made by the new president after the inauguration. In this speech, the president outlines some goals for the country.

How many times can a president be elected to office? Today, a president may be elected to office twice. Each term of office is four years. So a person may serve eight years in a row as president. This was decided by the 22nd Amendment in 1951.

Before 1951, there was no limit to the number of times a person could be elected to office. But only one president, Franklin Delano Roosevelt, was elected to three terms.

The 22nd Amendment was added to the Constitution, because many felt it was not a good idea for someone to

Speaker of the House, Tip O'Neill, and new vice-president, George Bush, watch as Ronald Reagan is sworn in as the 40th president of the United States.

be in office more than two terms. People were afraid that the president might become too powerful.

What if the president cannot finish a term? Sometimes, a president may not be able to finish a term. The president may die or become too ill to remain in office. In this case, the Constitution says who will become president.

The 25th Amendment to the Constitution set up some rules about this. It gives a way for Congress to remove a president who is too ill to stay in office.

This amendment also provides for the vice-president, who moves up to the office of the president, to appoint a new vice-president. If this happens, Congress must agree with the choice for the new vice-president.

9. The President as Chief Executive

Words to know	
Cabinet	officials
advisors	budget

The Constitution gives the president many jobs to do. The president is our country's chief executive. This means that the president must make sure that the laws of the country are carried out. As chief executive, the president has several powers.

What are the main powers of the president as chief executive? First, the president is in charge of all the offices in the executive branch. This includes the president's **Cabinet.**

The Cabinet is made up of people who help keep the president informed about the country's problems and needs. The people who serve on the Cabinet are called **advisors.**

The president is also in charge of the many offices and agencies of the government. Over three million people work for the federal government. It is a big job to watch over so many people.

Another power the president has as chief executive is to appoint federal **officials**. They include Cabinet members

and many other important members in government. The power to appoint people to important positions helps the president run the executive branch smoothly.

The president also writes executive orders. The president may use executive orders to help carry out laws. The country must follow these orders.

In 1979, President James Carter gave an executive order. He ordered that the temperature in most public buildings must be set at 78°F in the summer and 65°F in the winter. He gave this order to help save energy. Many people did not like this order, but it was obeyed.

Does the president have any other duties as chief executive? The president has two other duties as chief executive. He must put together a **budget.** A budget is a plan that tells how much money the country plans on spending. This is a very important decision. It affects every part of government.

Another important duty of the president is to report on how the country is doing. He does this in a speech called the State of the Union Address. This speech is made once a year to Congress.

The president talks about what has improved in the country. The problems and needs of the country are also talked about. The president may suggest ways to improve the country.

Today, it is not just Congress that hears this important speech. The State of the Union Address is carried by radio and TV stations. People from around the country and the world listen to this speech.

National Geographic Society photographer
courtesy U.S. Capitol Historical Society

President Reagan gives the State of the Union Address to Congress.

10. The President as Chief Legislator

The president must work closely with Congress. Congress makes the laws for our country. But the president plays a part in making laws. That is why the president is called the chief legislator. As chief legislator, the president has some more powers.

Does the president ever make new laws? The president does not make the country's laws. However, the president does write ideas for new laws. These ideas are given to Congress. Ideas for new laws are called **bills.**

At one time, just about all of the ideas for new laws came from the people in Congress. Today, senators and representatives still write many bills. But the president also suggests many ideas for new laws.

National Geographic Society photographer
courtesy U.S. Capitol Historical Society

The president signs a bill into law.

Sometimes, the president feels that a new law is very important. When this happens the president may go on radio or TV. Or the president may talk about ideas for new laws during the State of the Union Address. When the president does this, Congress pays special attention to the proposed law.

The job as chief legislator allows the president to have a major voice in the making of new laws and programs. This power helps the president to meet the country's goals.

Can the president ever say *no* to a new law? Sometimes, Congress tries to make a new law that the president does not like. If this happens, the president can **veto** it. This means he says *no* to it and refuses to sign it. If the president does not sign it, it does not become law.

However, this may not be the end. You will learn later what Congress can do if the president vetoes a bill.

How else does the president work with Congress? You have already learned that the president, as chief executive, can write executive orders. The president uses executive orders to help carry out laws. The president is often called upon to carry out the details of new laws.

Today, Congress is called upon to make many new laws. It must also start many new programs. Because of this, Congress only makes general laws. Then it is the president's duty to enforce the details of these laws.

The president also has the power to call Congress into session. When our country was young, Congress only met for a short time each year. So the president needed to be able to call Congress into session if something important happened.

The president still has the power to call Congress into session. But it is not used much today. Today, Congress has so much work to do, it meets almost all year long.

President Reagan addresses a joint session of Congress.

11. The President as Chief Diplomat

Words to know	
foreign policy	recognize
treaties	

The president is the spokesman for our country. To be a spokesman means to speak for someone else. The president speaks for the whole country when dealing with other countries. The president is our country's chief diplomat.

What does the president do as the spokesman for our country? Often, the president will travel to other countries. The president will meet with world leaders. These visits are important. They help keep peace among the nations of the world. Helping to keep the nations of the world at peace is part of the president's job as chief diplomat.

The president also decides if the United States will work or help another country. All of these decisions are part of our country's **foreign policy**. Foreign policy is how we feel about the rest of the world. A country's foreign policy will sometimes decide between war and peace.

What else does the president do as chief diplomat? The president can

President Carter and General Omar Torrijos sign the Panama Canal treaties.

Chinese Premier Zhao Ziyang replies to the greeting he has received from President Reagan.

make **treaties** with other countries. Treaties are agreements. They may be about many things. They can be about giving money to help a poor country, or about not sending troops into certain parts of the world. Sometimes, treaties can be used to make peace among countries.

The president is the only person who can sign a treaty for the United States. But most treaties need to be approved by the Senate.

In 1978, President James Carter signed two treaties with Panama. These treaties gave control of the Panama Canal to Panama. Many people did not like the treaties. Others felt the treaties were good. After many long talks, the Senate approved both treaties.

Does the president have the power to recognize new governments? Yes, the president can **recognize** new governments. This means he must decide if a country's government is the lawful representative of its people. Sometimes, a country's government may be overthrown. In this case, the president must decide if the new government should be recognized.

In 1981, China was recognized by the United States. China's government had existed for many years. But the United States had never recognized it. President Carter finally recognized China. The process of recognizing the Chinese government began under President Nixon. It was a long process.

Once a country is recognized by the president it can get much help from the United States. Agreements can be made between the countries. These agreements help to keep the United States and other countries on friendly terms. If a country is not recognized, then these agreements cannot be made.

12. The President as Commander-in-Chief

> **Words to know**
>
> civilian   armed forces
> wages

The writer of the Constitution wanted the head of the military to be a **civilian**. A civilian is someone who is not a member of the military. The president of the United States is a civilian. The writers of the Constitution decided to make the president the commander-in-chief of the **armed forces** (military).

Today, the president has much more military power than the writers of the Constitution planned. These powers have come about as presidents have had to act during times of war.

What are the president's duties as commander-in-chief? As commander-in-chief the president has many duties. He must:

- lead all federal and state armed forces.
- decide on a defense policy.
- suggest a defense budget.
- appoint leaders of the armed forces.
- direct where the armed forces will be in the world.
- carry out all laws having to do with defense.
- direct all war efforts.

Can the president declare war? No, the president cannot declare war. Only Congress can do this. However, the president can sometimes send troops into a country without declaring war. This has happened several times. In fact, there have been wars fought without declaring war. This was true for both the Korean and Vietnam wars.

Even without a state of war, the president must protect the lives of United States citizens in other countries. The president can use troops to do this.

What is the War Powers Act? Many people have been concerned that the president has too much military power as commander-in-chief. They have been especially concerned that the president is able to send troops into a country without Congress declaring war.

Congress passed the War Powers Act in 1974. This act allows the president to send the military into a country for only 60 days. After this time, Congress must approve the president's actions. Also, Congress can stop troops from going into a country at anytime.

Does the president have any special powers during a war? Yes, during a war the president has some special powers. War is a time of emergency or great need. In emergencies people sometimes have to act quickly.

When the country is at war, the president may have to act quickly. Decisions may need to be made fast. The president would have to act for the whole country.

The president's powers during war include:

- placing limits on **wages** (money earned for doing a job) and prices.
- rationing food, clothing, and other items.
- controlling all industry that is war related.
- suspending personal freedoms.

There are limits to what the president can do though. Congress still has to approve the president's actions.

The defense of the United States is very important. It is up to the president to decide much of that defense policy.

Ernest J. Larsen, Jr.

The military uses training exercises to prepare its men and women. These exercises may include mock battles or other emergencies.

13. The President as Chief Jurist

The president also works closely with the judicial branch. That is why the president is also called the chief jurist. As chief jurist the president:

- appoints judges to federal courts.
- appoints lawyers for the government in federal cases.
- grants **pardons** and issues **amnesty** orders.

The Constitution gives these powers to the president as chief jurist.

What is a pardon? A pardon is a legal document that excuses or forgives someone for doing something.

The president has three choices when granting a pardon. A full pardon can be given. Then it is as if the action the president is forgiving never happened. Or the president can shorten or make a **sentence** less severe. A sentence is the punishment someone receives for a crime. Lastly, the president can choose to postpone a sentence. No one can cancel the president's pardon.

Can the president grant pardons in all court cases? No, the president cannot grant pardons in all court cases. The president can only grant pardons in federal cases. (A federal case is a case about a federal law.)

In 1974, President Gerald Ford used his power as chief jurist to pardon former President Richard Nixon. Many people believed that President Nixon had committed crimes while he was president.

What's the difference between a pardon and an order of amnesty? Amnesty is a pardon granted to a large group of people.

During the Vietnam war many men went to Canada so they would not be sent to fight. The law said that if you were called, you had to go. Rather than obey this law many men left the country. After the war was over many men wanted to return to the United States.

In 1977, President James Carter granted amnesty to these men. That meant they could return without being punished. President Carter decided to grant amnesty to these men because he felt there were already too many bad feelings about the war. He hoped that by letting the men return, Americans would more quickly forget about the war.

President Nixon decided to leave office. Many thought he should stand trial. However, President Ford used his power as chief jurist to pardon Nixon of any crimes he might have committed. The photo above shows President Nixon in happier times. He is waving to the crowds as he boards Air Force One on his first overseas trip as president.

14. The Role of the Vice-President

Word to know
resign

The vice-president is the second most important person in our government. As you have learned, if anything were to happen to the president, the vice-president would become president.

Who can be vice-president? The Constitution states the same rules for vice-president as for president. Thus, the vice-president must:

- be a citizen born in this country.
- be at least 35 years old.
- be a resident of the United States for 14 years.

What are the duties of the vice-president? The Constitution only says that the vice-president should sit in charge of the Senate. This is why the vice-president is called the president of the Senate.

Many vice-presidents have felt that this job was not important enough. Recently, many more jobs have been given to the vice-president. The vice-president usually attends meetings of the president's Cabinet. The vice-president is a member of the National Security Council and is in charge of many important committees.

When would the vice-president take over as president? The vice-president would take over as the president if:

- the president should die.
- the president should **resign** (choose to leave office) or be removed from office.
- the president is too ill to do the job well.

Have any vice-presidents ever taken over as president? Yes. Eight presidents have died in office. In each case, the vice-president became president. One president, Richard Nixon, resigned. When he did this the vice-president became president.

While Nixon was president he had to choose a new vice-president. Spiro Agnew, his vice-president, resigned. Nixon chose Gerald Ford to replace Agnew. Then Nixon resigned. Ford became president. President Ford had to choose a new vice-president. He chose Nelson Rockefeller. For the first time in history, the country had an unelected president and vice-president.

Unit 2 Summary

The executive branch of our government is made up of the president, and the president's advisors and staff. The executive branch is large. There are over three million people who work for the federal government.

The president and the vice-president are elected to office. When people vote for president and vice-president they are really voting for electors. The electors then vote for president and vice-president.

The president has five important jobs. These are: chief executive, chief legislator, chief diplomat, commander-in-chief, and chief jurist. To do these jobs, the president has many duties and powers. These include:

- carrying out the nation's laws.
- giving Congress ideas for new laws.
- deciding on foreign policy.
- deciding on military defense.
- making a budget for the country.
- granting pardons and amnesty.

The vice-president is an important part of our government. He is called the president of the Senate. He is in charge of some very important committees. The vice-president becomes president if the president becomes ill, dies in office, or resigns.

UNIT 3

The President's Helpers

The president and vice-president are not the only members of the executive branch. The president has a Cabinet. The Cabinet is part of the executive branch.

The members of the Cabinet help the president. They help the president in many ways. They advise the president. They gather information for the president. They also make sure that the president's decisions are carried out.

The Cabinet is a very important part of the executive branch. Each Cabinet member heads an executive department. Today, there are 13 executive departments.

The executive branch also includes many independent agencies. These agencies help to protect the rights of people.

How does the Cabinet help the president? What are the 13 executive departments? How do independent agencies help people? You will learn the answers to all these questions in this unit.

By the end of this unit you should be able to:

- know what the Cabinet is.
- explain the duties of the executive departments.
- know two kinds of independent agencies.
- explain how independent agencies affect you.

15. An Overview of the Cabinet

> **Words to know**
>
> expires   secretaries
> attorney

The president has many jobs to do. To do these jobs well, the president has advisors. These advisors are usually experts in a certain area. These advisors form the president's Cabinet.

What does the Cabinet do? The Cabinet helps the president in many ways. The members of the Cabinet advise the president. They gather information for the president. They also make sure that the president's decisions are carried out. The Cabinet is an important part of the executive branch.

How many Cabinet members are there? In 1789, Congress set up only three executive departments to help the president. They were the Department of State, the Department of War, and the Department of the Treasury. As our country grew, more departments were needed.

Today, there are 13 executive departments. So there are 13 Cabinet members.

How are Cabinet members chosen? The president carefully chooses each Cabinet member. It is an important job. It carries much power.

Cabinet members often share the same ideas as the president. Also, they are usually members of the same political party as the president. Cabinet members may often be from different parts of the country.

The president chooses Cabinet members. But the Senate must approve the president's choices. If the Senate does not approve the president's choice, then the president must choose a different person. It is very rare that the Senate would not approve the president's choices though.

How long does a Cabinet member serve? A Cabinet member may serve until the president's term **expires** (comes to an end). The president may fire a Cabinet member. A Cabinet member may also resign.

Cabinet Member		Executive Department
Secretary of State	is the head of	the Department of State
Secretary of Treasury	is the head of	the Treasury Department
Secretary of Defense	is the head of	the Department of Defense
Attorney General	is the head of	the Department of Justice
Secretary of Interior	is the head of	the Department of Interior
Secretary of Agriculture	is the head of	the Department of Agriculture
Secretary of Commerce	is the head of	the Department of Commerce
Secretary of Labor	is the head of	the Department of Labor
Secretary of Health and Human Services	is the head of	the Department of Health and Human Services
Secretary of Housing and Urban Development	is the head of	the Department of Housing and Urban Development
Secretary of Transportation	is the head of	the Department of Transportation
Secretary of Energy	is the head of	the Department of Energy
Secretary of Education	is the head of	the Department of Education

What are the 13 executive departments? Look at the chart above. It shows the 13 executive departments. It also shows which Cabinet member heads the department. Notice that most Cabinet members are referred to as **secretaries.** This is their title.

One Cabinet member is not called a secretary. That person is called the Attorney General. **Attorney** is another word for lawyer. The Attorney General is the country's lawyer.

16. The Department of State

Words to know	
ambassador	passport
embassy	

The Department of State is a very important executive department. It was one of the first executive departments created by Congress.

Who is the head of the Department of State? The head of the Department of State is the Secretary of State. The Secretary of State is an important person in our government. The Secretary of State advises the president on foreign policy.

What does the Department of State do? The Department of State works to keep peace between the United States and other countries. It forms a link between the United States and other nations. It tells other countries about the kind of agreements the president would like to make with them.

The president and the Secretary of State meet with officials from many countries. Sometimes, the Secretary of State meets alone with foreign officials. In that case, the Secretary of State would represent the president.

Does the Department of State send representatives to other countries? Yes, the Department of State often sends representatives to other countries. These representatives talk with the leaders and representatives of other nations. Once the United States recognizes a country, a representative is usually sent to that country. This kind of representative is called an **ambassador**. The ambassador may live in a special place in that country. This is called an **embassy.** The United States has many embassies throughout the world.

Does the Department of State send representatives to the United Nations? Yes, our representative to the United Nations is sent by the Department of State. The United Nations meets in New York City. There, our representative meets with representatives from many countries. Together they try to take care of the world's problems peacefully.

How does the Department of State affect you? Have you ever traveled to a foreign country? To do this, you would need a **passport.** This is a document that says you are a citizen of the United States. It is the Department of State who issues passports to people.

UPI/Bettmann Archive

The General Assembly of the United Nations opens a new session with moment of silence. 157 nations are members of the U.N.

17. The Departments of Defense and Justice

Words to know	
recruited	immigration
investigate	immigrants

The Departments of Defense and Justice are also important executive departments.

The Department of Defense was set up in 1947. The Secretary of Defense advises the president on the military.

The Department of Justice makes sure that all federal laws are enforced (carried out).

What are some of the duties of the Secretary of Defense? The Secretary of Defense watches over our national defense. Money for the military must be set aside. Military supplies have to be ordered. Military weapons have to be built. Men and women have to be **recruited** for the military. The Secretary of Defense must make sure that all these things are done well.

In times of war, the Secretary of Defense becomes very important. This is because the Secretary of Defense watches over all the armed forces.

Does Congress have any control over the Department of Defense? Yes, Congress has some control over the Department of Defense. Sometimes, Congress does not approve of all the money the Department of Defense wants to spend. Then Congress and the Department of Defense must compromise.

What does the Attorney General do? The Attorney General advises the president on our federal laws. The Attorney General also represents the country in cases before federal courts.

Does the Department of Justice do anything else? Yes, the Department of Justice has many duties. One duty is to watch over federal prisons. Another is to **investigate** (look into) when federal laws are broken. There is a special part of the Justice Department that does the investigating. It is called the Federal Bureau of Investigation (FBI).

The Justice Department also enforces laws concerning **immigration**. That is, it watches over laws about people from other countries who want to live in the United States.

Remember that people from all over the world settled in the United States. We are a land of **immigrants.**

U.S. Dept. of Justice

This agent practices shooting at the FBI Academy in Virginia.

New York Historical Society

For many people America was a place to build a new life. This engraving shows people waiting on docks for ships to take them to New York City.

18. The Departments of Commerce and Agriculture

```
Words to know

commerce    census
```

The Department of Commerce and the Department of Agriculture are two more executive departments.

What does the Department of Commerce do? The Department of Commerce has many jobs. **Commerce** means trade. People trade products for money or for other products. So the Department of Commerce watches over the country's businesses.

The Secretary of Commerce advises the president on the country's business matters. The Secretary of Commerce also helps to improve business between the United States and other countries.

Does the Department of Commerce do anything else? Yes, it does do some other things. The Department of Commerce gives loans to small businesses. It reports on the weather across the country. It is also in charge of taking the **census** every ten years. Every ten years, it counts the number of people living in the United States.

As you can see, the Department of Commerce does many different things.

What are the duties of the Department of Agriculture? The Department of Agriculture helps our farmers. It helps farmers grow better crops and raise healthy animals. It also watches over farm prices and products.

Does the Department of Agriculture affect people not living on a farm? Yes, the Department of Agriculture affects everyone. It even affects you if you live in a large city.

Did you eat lunch at school today? The Department of Agriculture oversees school lunch programs. It makes sure school lunches are healthy.

Does your family grow a garden? The Department of Agriculture gives out information on how to grow a good garden. It will also tell you how to keep food fresh for a long time.

Did you eat some meat today? The Department of Agriculture sends people to inspect the meat we eat. These people make sure the meat is healthy.

The Department of Agriculture tries to help Americans eat right. Food products have labels to tell us what they contain. The Department of Agriculture also tells us what kinds of food to eat each day to stay healthy.

19. The Departments of Interior and Energy

Words to know

natural resources   nuclear

The Department of the Interior oversees the country's land and **natural resources**. Natural resources are the things around us that have value. Water and air are natural resources. So are minerals and metals. Animals and plants are natural resources, too. Some natural resources such as coal, help us produce energy. It's the job of the Department of Energy to watch over energy.

How does the Department of the Interior watch over natural resources? The Secretary of the Interior's job is to advise the president on how federal land should be used. Some is set aside for national parks. Other land is set aside for wildlife. And still other land is used for development.

Does the Department of the Interior do anything else? Another job of the Department of the Interior is to watch over Native Americans. It advises the president on problems such as housing or education that Native Americans might have.

Is the Department of Energy very old? No, the Department of Energy is

One of the cooling towers at Three Mile Island nuclear power plant.

not very old. It was started in 1977 by President Carter.

What's the purpose of the Department of Energy? The purpose of the Department of Energy is to make sure the country has enough energy. It watches over all the ways of getting energy. This includes electrical, gas, coal, solar, **nuclear**, and other forms of energy.

The Department of Energy also watches over the cost of energy. It also looks for new ways that we might get energy. It also tries to find ways to keep the country from wasting too much energy.

20. The Departments of the Treasury and Labor

Words to know

employed   interest

The Treasury Department watches over the country's money. This is a large job. The Department of Labor watches over the working conditions of **employed** (working) people. This is a large job, too.

How does the Treasury Department watch over the country's money? First, the Treasury Department is in charge of making the country's money. It makes all the country's coin and paper money.

Second, the Treasury Department watches over the federal government's money. It is the Treasury Department who pays the government's bills. Billions of dollars are handled each year by the Treasury Department.

Where does the money used by the Treasury Department come from? Money comes into the Treasury Department from many places. This money helps to run our country. Much of the money comes from taxes. Other money comes from selling things such as stamps.

Does the Treasury Department ever run out of money? Yes, the Treasury Department does run out of money. Sometimes when this happens, the federal government will borrow

These people are standing in line to apply for unemployment benefits.

money. Our federal government borrows billions of dollars each year. This money and a little extra (called **interest**) must be repaid.

What does the Department of Labor do? The Department of Labor makes sure that everyone is paid a proper wage. A wage is the money earned for doing a job.

The Department of Labor also gathers job information and sets up programs that train people who lack job skills.

It also helps people who are unemployed (not working).

The Secretary of Labor reports to the president about any labor problems in the country.

Is it the Department of Labor that makes people wear hard hats when working in dangerous places? Yes, the Department of Labor watches over the places people work.

The Department of Labor can make people wear certain clothes when they are employed at certain jobs. It sets up safety rules. Sometimes this means wearing hard hats. Sometimes this means wearing a mask.

How else does the Department of Labor affect you? The Department of Labor reports every month on how many people are not employed. It also tells people which jobs are most in demand. This gives people an idea of what kind of job to look for. This information helps students to make wise choices about the kind of skills they should learn.

Rick Bagley

This welder wears special safety clothing and equipment to protect him on the job.

21. The Department of Health and Human Services

The Department of Health and Human Services performs many services for people. It has a large affect on everyone in the country.

What are some of the duties of the Department of Health and Human Services? The Department of Health and Human Services has many duties. It advises the president on federal health programs. These include child care, family health, and programs for the elderly. Programs for disabled persons are also watched over by this department.

The safety of food and drugs we buy is watched over by the Department of Health and Human Services. It also has programs about the abuse of drugs and alcohol.

What is the social security system? The **social security** system is part of the Department of Health and Human Services. Most people who earn over $400 a year pay money into social security.

The federal government collects money from social security. It puts it into a special trust fund. The money is used to pay benefits to disabled people. People who are retired receive some money from social security. Sometimes, social security will give money to the family of a person who dies.

The main purpose of the social security system is to make sure that people are cared for once they are no longer able to work.

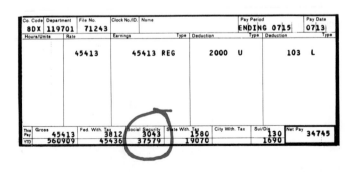

22. The Department of Education

Word to know

vocational

The Department of Education is a very large executive department. It watches over many federal education programs. The Secretary of Education advises the president on how well the people of our country are being educated.

How does the Department of Education affect you? The Department of Education affects everyone who goes to school. It often provides schools with money to help provide special classes.

Many adults learn to read and write in adult education classes.

Does your school have a **vocational** training program? Vocational programs teach job skills. They include skills such as learning how to repair a car. Money for these kinds of programs often comes from the federal government.

Do you know someone who is taking an adult education class? These programs help adults learn to read and write. Much money for adult education comes from the federal government.

Does the Department of Education affect how your school is run? The answer to this is both yes and no. States make many of the decisions having to do with education. How long you must go to school is decided by your state.

But the Department of Education may have some control over your school. As you have just learned, many schools get federal money for special programs. The Department of Education has a say on how this money is spent.

23. The Departments of HUD and Transportation

There are two more executive departments left in the Cabinet. One is the Department of Housing and Urban Development (HUD). The other is the Department of Transportation.

What is the job of HUD? The Department of Housing and Urban Development does just what its name says. It watches over the country's housing programs. It gives money to help improve **urban** areas. These are city areas. It also gives money to build homes for older and poor people.

HUD tries to improve the country's cities. It is the job of the Secretary of HUD to report to the president on the problems of our country's cities. The Secretary must also advise the president on the country's housing needs.

What is the job of the Department of Transportation? The Department of Transportation oversees the country's many forms of transportation. It gives money for highways between states. It may also pay for improvements to railroads and waterways.

Money from HUD may go to build apartments for people who would not be able to afford such housing otherwise.

Was it the Department of Transportation who put seat belts in cars? Yes, the Department of Transportation was the one who had seat belts put in cars. One of this department's jobs is to make sure that transportation is safe. Putting seat belts in cars is just one example of how the Department of Transportation tries to make your life safer.

Does the Department of Transportation investigate major accidents? Yes, this department may investigate major accidents such as a plane crash. The Federal Aviation Administration (FAA) is part of the Department of Transportation. It is the FAA's job to investigate plane crashes.

The FAA tries to find out the causes of accidents. It hopes to be able to prevent other accidents by doing this. Sometimes new laws are made to make travel safer. Float seats in airplanes are an example of this.

Most states require small children to ride in special safety seats.

Does the Department of Transportation make all the safety rules? No, the Department of Transportation does not make all the safety rules. Sometimes, states have their own rules for travel. One example of this is the use of an infant car seat. Many states have laws that say that small children must have a safety seat.

The FAA works to make air travel safer.

24. Independent Agencies

You have learned that there are 13 executive departments. These 13 departments are part of the executive branch. The executive branch also includes many independent agencies. They are not a part of the president's Cabinet, though.

Have independent agencies always been a part of our government? Independent agencies have not always been a part of our government. The United States Constitution did not set up independent agencies. Independent agencies were begun during the last 100 years.

Why were independent agencies begun? Independent agencies were begun to protect people's health and money. Before independent agencies were begun, people had to protect their own rights. Not much could be done if a large company was not fair to others.

What happened to cause independent agencies to be set up? Many new companies were begun after the Civil War. These companies were very large. Small business people and farmers felt that these large companies needed to be **regulated** (controlled). They wanted to be sure that they were treated fairly by the large companies.

When was the first independent agency begun? In 1887, Congress began the Interstate Commerce Commisssion (ICC). A **commission** is another type of agency. The ICC was begun to regulate train **freight** among states. (Freight is something that is transported from one place to another. Another word for freight is cargo.)

Does the president have much control over independent agencies? Remember, independent agencies are not like executive departments. The president has much control over executive departments. The president does not have direct control of independent agencies.

American Steamship Co.

Ore tankers are common on the Great Lakes.

For this reason, independent agencies are sometimes called the fourth branch of the federal government. This means that they are one more way that the powers of government are divided. But independent agencies are not really a fourth branch. They are part of the executive branch.

Is there only one kind of independent agency? No, there are two kinds of independent agencies. One kind is called a regulatory agency. The other kind is called a service agency. Both kinds have special duties.

What is the difference between regulatory and service agencies? Some independent agencies make sure that certain federal laws are obeyed. Regulatory agencies may also make new regulations. These regulations are like laws. They must be followed.

Service agencies do a service for the country. They do not regulate.

25. Regulatory Agencies

Words to know	
communications	competition
quasi	environment
advertising	consumer

Independent regulatory agencies have a **quasi**-judicial role. This means they have some judicial powers. They are able to make regulations for companies and people to follow. They can also decide if certain laws have been broken. There are several regulatory agencies.

What are some important regulatory agencies? An important regulatory agency is the Federal Reserve System. The Federal Reserve System is the nation's bank. It was started in 1913. It regulates the flow of money in the country. The job of the Federal Reserve System is to make sure United States banks stay strong.

As you have already learned, the ICC regulates transportation among the states. It is a very important agency. It tries to watch over the quality of service given to people.

Does a regulatory agency watch over communications? Yes, the Federal Communications Commission (FCC) regulates **communications.** This means it watches over radio, television, wire, and cable. It also gives permission for TV and radio stations to be on the air.

Who protects the environment? The Environmental Protection Agency (EPA) protects the **environment.** The environment is the world around us. The EPA's job is to control all types of pollution. The EPA works with state and local governments.

What does the Federal Trade Commission (FTC) do? The job of this agency is to make sure there is free trade in the United States. There should be fair **competition** among businesses. This means that businesses who sell the same service or goods will compete with each other. The FTC must also make sure that all **advertising** is true. This includes advertising of food, drugs, and cosmetics. Advertising tries to persuade you to buy something. Ads are found on billboards, and in newspapers and magazines. Ads, called commercials, are on TV and radio, too.

Is there an agency that watches over the products people buy? Yes, the Consumer Product Safety Commission watches over **consumer** products. A consumer is anyone who buys or uses a product. This commission makes regulations so products are safe to use. To do this, the Consumer Product Safety Commission sets safety standards. This agency also investigates if a product causes injury, illness, or death.

Are there other agencies that protect the health and safety of people? Yes, there are agencies that protect people. One is the Nuclear Regulatory Commission. It regulates the use of nuclear energy. It has the power to inspect nuclear power plants to make sure they are safe. It does this to protect the health and safety of people.

Billboards like this can be found all across the country.

26. Independent Service Agencies

Independent service agencies do not regulate. Instead, these agencies perform a service for the federal government.

Does your bank have a FDIC sign on its door? If so, this means that the money in the bank is **insured** by the Federal Deposit Insurance Corporation (FDIC). The FDIC makes sure that money you put in the bank is safe and will be returned to you.

What is another service agency? Another service agency is ACTION. ACTION oversees all federal **volunteer** programs. People who serve in volunteer programs do not receive a wage. They give, or volunteer, their time and services to help others.

ACTION supports self-help efforts of low-income people. It includes volunteer groups such as VISTA, Foster Grandparents, Drug Abuse Prevention Programs, and the Retired Senior Volunteer Program.

What is NASA? NASA stands for the National Aeronautics and Space Administration program. NASA's duty is to look into ways to use space for peaceful purposes. This means building space transportation. It also means learning more about space.

What is the Selective Service System? The Selective Service System makes sure that there are enough people in the military. During some years there has been a military draft. The draft meant that men had to join the military. The Selective Service set up the draft.

Is there an agency to help small businesses? Yes, there is an agency to help small businesses. It is the Small Business Administration (SBA). It gives information on how to run a small business. It also gives loans to small businesses. These loans are for helping a small business to get started. Loans are also given to help a small business that has been hurt by such things as fire or floods.

Is the United States Postal Service an independent service agency? Yes, the Postal Service is an independent service agency. This large agency makes sure that the country's mail is delivered.

Unit 3 Summary

The president is the head of the executive branch. The president has many jobs to do. To help the president do these jobs well, the president has some helpers. Some of the president's most important helpers are in the executive departments. There are 13 executive departments. The head of these executive departments form the president's Cabinet.

The president's Cabinet is a very important part of our government. It advises the president on the country's problems. Cabinet members may also suggest ideas to improve or change things in the country.

Members of the Cabinet are appointed by the president. They may serve for as long as the president is in office. The Senate must approve the president's choices for the Cabinet.

The 13 executive departments affect Americans in many ways. The president's Cabinet has much power in our government.

Independent agencies are also a part of the executive branch. You have learned about two kinds of agencies: regulatory agencies and service agencies.

Independent agencies were begun to protect the rights of people and businesses. People may write or call the office of an independent agency. They may ask the agency for help. Independent agencies are an important part of our federal government. They are here to help you.

The Legislative Branch

The legislative branch of the federal government is called Congress. The job of Congress is to make the laws for our country. Congress is made up of two parts: the House of Representatives and the Senate.

The men who wrote our Constitution were not sure how to set up the executive branch. They did not want the president to have too much power. On the other hand, the writers of the Constitution knew exactly how they wanted to set up the legislative branch.

They divided Congress into two houses. They did this for three reasons. First, our Constitution was built on the English system of government. This system has two lawmaking houses. Second, a one-house lawmaking system had been tried. This system had not worked very well. Third, the writers wanted to have each house as a check on the activities of the other house.

The two houses of Congress today share great powers as the lawmaking branch of our government. The 535 men and women who are elected to Congress must know about the country's problems. They must be able to change laws or make new laws to help solve the country's problems.

How are new laws made? What are the powers given to Congress? What powers has Congress gained through history? By reading Unit 4 you will learn the answers to these questions.

By the end of this unit you should be able to:

- list ten powers of Congress.
- explain how a law is made.

27. The Two Houses of Congress

The making of new laws is one of the main jobs of our government. Both houses of Congress take part in making these new laws.

One house of Congress is called the Senate. The other house is called the House of Representatives. Members of the Senate are called senators. Members of the House of Representatives are called representatives. Both senators and representatives are elected to Congress to represent the people of their state.

Who elects the members of Congress? The people directly elect all members of Congress. This was set up by the 17th Amendment to the Constitution. This amendment was passed in 1913. Before the 17th Amendment, members of the Senate were elected by state legislatures.

Look at the chart below. It shows who can be elected to the Senate and the House of Representatives. It also shows how long each serves.

How long does Congress meet? A new Congress meets on January 3 of every odd numbered year. The first Congress met in 1789. In 1985, the 99th Congress will meet. The life of Congress is only two years. This is because representatives are elected every two years.

There are two sessions to every term of Congress. One session lasts

A Senator must:	A Representative must:
• be 30 years old.	• be 25 years old.
• be a citizen for 9 years.	• be a citizen for 7 years.
• live in state representing.	• live in state representing.
A Senator:	**A Representative:**
• serves for 6 years.	• serves for 2 years.
• has no limit to the number of terms that can be served.	• has no limit to the number of terms that can be served.

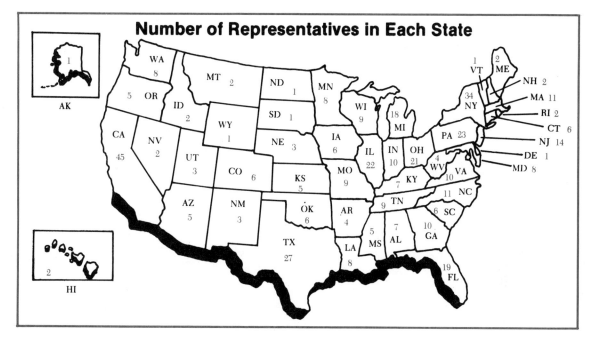

Number of Representatives in Each State

AK 1

WA 8
OR 5
MT 2
ND 1
MN 8
VT 1
ME 2
NH 2
MA 11
NY 34
ID 2
SD 1
WI 9
MI 18
RI 2
CT 6
NJ 14
DE 1
MD 8
WY 1
IA 6
IL 22
IN 10
OH 21
PA 23
NV 2
UT 3
CO 6
NE 3
KS 5
MO 9
KY 7
WV 4
VA 10
CA 45
AZ 5
NM 3
OK 6
AR 4
TN 9
NC 11
SC 6
TX 27
LA 8
MS 5
AL 7
GA 10
FL 19

HI 2

one year. The members of Congress may take time off for holidays, important business trips, vacations, and for campaigning.

Remember how the large and small states argued during the constitutional convention? The large and small states argued over how they were to be represented in Congress. They ended their argument by deciding to compromise. Their compromise was written into the Constitution. The Consitution decides how each state will be represented in Congress.

The Constitution says that each state must have two senators. This gives each state equal representation in the Senate. There are 100 senators.

The Constitution also says that the number of representatives a state has in the House depends on the number of people in that state. The House of Representatives gives states with more people more representation.

This is the compromise that the large and small states agreed to. It has become part of our law.

How is the number of people living in each state decided? Every ten years the number of people in each state is counted. This is called taking a census. The number of people in each state decides the number of **districts** the state will have. Each district must have about the same number of people.

After it is decided how many districts each state will have, each state is divided into districts. Sometimes, a state will gain districts. Sometimes, a state will lose districts. It all depends on how many people live in the state. The number of representatives for each state equals the number of districts for each state. Today, each representative in the House speaks for about 500,000 people.

Look at the map above. Find the state you live in. How many representatives does your state have?

28. The Lawmaking Powers of Congress

> **Words to know**
>
> expressed power   implied power

The men who wrote the Constitution wanted Congress to be the most powerful branch of our government. They gave Congress many different lawmaking powers. No other branch of our government was given the power to make laws for our country.

Congress has two kinds of lawmaking powers. These two powers are called expressed and implied powers.

What is an expressed power? An **expressed power** is written for an exact purpose. Each power states exactly what Congress can do. Most of Congress' lawmaking powers are expressed powers. They cover areas such as trade, money, the courts, the post office, and defense.

What are the expressed powers given to Congress? The expressed powers of Congress include:

- the power to collect taxes and pay the nation's bills.
- the power to borrow money.
- the power to control trade with other countries.
- the power to allow people from foreign countries to become citizens.
- the power to print money.
- the power to make laws to punish people who print phony money.
- the power to set places for post offices.
- the power to protect the written work and inventions of individuals.
- the power to create new courts.
- the power to set laws for crimes committed at sea.
- the power to declare war.
- the power to gather an army.
- the power to support a navy.
- the power to set laws for the army and navy.
- the power to make laws for the District of Columbia.

When the Consitution was written, the U.S. did not have an air force. (Remember, the airplane hadn't been invented yet!) However, Congress' implied power gave it the power to create an air force once there was the need for one.

What is an implied power? A power not written for an exact purpose is an **implied power**. It is a general power. The last power the Constitution gives to Congress is an implied power.

What does the implied power of Congress say? The implied power says that Congress may make any needed new laws. In other words, Congress may make any law it feels is necessary to carry out its expressed powers.

The implied power of Congress is a very general power. It may be used in many different ways.

Are there certain powers that Congress does not have? Yes, the Constitution states what powers Congress does not have. Congress may not pass any laws that are unfair to any one person or group. In other words, all laws must treat people equally.

29. The Non-lawmaking Powers of Congress

Today, Congress has much more power than the writers of the Constitution had planned. This is because the country has more people and because life is more complex today. When the Constitution was written we did not have large cities. We did not have a need for mass transportation. During the time when the Constitutuion was written each state took care of most of the people's problems.

Today, we have many more people spread throughout the country. The country is also larger. As the country has grown, Congress has gained more power. Today, many of the country's problems are helped by laws made by Congress.

Congress' main powers are for making our laws. But Congress has other powers, too. These other powers are called non-lawmaking powers.

What are the non-lawmaking powers of Congress? Congress has five important non-lawmaking powers. These are:

- impeachment
- approving federal officials
- investigation
- approval of money spent by the federal government
- suggesting amendments to the Constitution.

Who can Congress impeach? Only the House of Representatives has the power of impeachment. To impeach means to bring charges against someone. If someone is impeached it means there is reason to believe that the person has committed a crime.

The House can impeach any federal official. Even the president can be impeached.

After the House of Representatives has voted to impeach a federal official, the Senate holds a trial. The chief justice of the Supreme Court **presides** at (oversees) the trial. Any federal official found guilty by the Senate of impeachment charges is removed from office.

Which federal officials must the Senate approve? The Senate approves many federal officials named by the president. This includes the people in the president's Cabinet, ambassadors, federal judges, and many others.

Who decides how federal funds are spent? Congress has the power of approval over federal funds. This means Congress has the final say on how the federal government's money is spent. Congress also decides on whether federal taxes should be lower or higher. This is an important power of Congress. You will learn more about how the federal government collects and spends money in Chapter 10.

Why does Congress have investigative power? The members of Congress must know about the problems in the country. To do this, Congress has the power to investigate. It can look into or investigate many areas such as crime, drugs, car safety, and others. Congress can also investigate the activities of federal officials. It can investigate the way federal programs are carried out.

During an investigation many people are asked to speak to Congress. This helps the members of Congress hear different ideas. Sometimes new laws are made after the investigation of a problem.

Sheperd Sherbell/The Picture Group

George Shultz speaks to Congress during the hearing to see whether Congress will approve him as President Reagan's choice for Secretary of State.

30. A Special Power of Congress

The Constitution gives Congress a very special power. This is the power to change the Constitution. Congress does this by writing an amendment.

Amendments change the Constitution. Usually, they set new rights for people. Today, there are 26 amendments to the Constitution.

It is not easy to pass an amendment to the Constitution. There are two ways: the legislative and convention methods. However, the legislative method has been used every time except once.

How does the legislative method work? Under the legislative method, both the Senate and the House must vote on a proposed amendment. At least two-thirds of the members of both houses must vote *yes* to the proposed amendment.

The proposed amendment is then sent to the state legislatures. Three-fourths of all the state legislatures must vote *yes* on the proposed amendment. The amendment does not pass if three-fourths of the states do not vote *yes*. A state legislature can also later change its vote. If the proposed amendment is

adopted (approved) by three-fourths of the states, it becomes part of the Constitution.

What is the convention method? The convention method is the second way the Constitution can be amended. This means that every state must call a convention to amend the Constitution. For an amendment to be passed, three-fourths of the conventions have to vote *yes*.

The convention method for amending the Constitution has only been used once. This was to **repeal** (do away with) another amendment.

In 1919, the 19th Amendment was passed. This amendment banned the use and sale of **alcoholic** drinks. Alcoholic drinks include any sort of liquor, wine, or beer. Many people were unhappy with this amendment. They felt the government had no right telling people what they could or couldn't drink.

What is the Bill of Rights? As you've already learned, the Bill of Rights is the first ten amendments to the Constitution. The Bill of Rights was added to the Constitution in 1791. It was added by the writers of the Constitution. It was the promise of writing a Bill of Rights that helped get the Constitution passed at the convention. Many people were afraid of a strong government, and they wanted to be sure that their rights would be protected.

What does the Bill of Rights say? The Bill of Rights is a list of freedoms that all citizens have. The Bill of Rights says we have the freedom to:

- worship as we choose.
- speak freely.
- have a free press.
- form groups for peaceful reasons.
- speak to the government.
- have a speedy and fair trial.

What do some of the other amendments say? Sixteen more amendments have been added to the Constitution since the Bill of Rights. All these amendments are important. Look at the chart below. It shows the 11th through 26th Amendments.

Are there any plans today to add another amendment to the Constitution? Yes, there are many people today who would like to see a 27th Amendment to the Constitution. This proposed amendment has become known as the Equal Rights Amendment (ERA).

Many people are concerned that women have not been treated as equally as men. They argue that the only way to stop unfair treatment is to make it a law. Although many people are for ERA, more states need to vote for it before the amendment will be passed.

Amendments since the Bill of Rights

The 11th Amendment:	prevents a person from suing a state he doesn't live in.
The 12th Amendment:	changed the way the president and vice-president were elected.
The 13th Amendment:	did away with slavery.
The 14th Amendment:	made former slaves citizens. It also states how someone becomes a citizen.
The 15th Amendment:	says that people cannot be denied the right to vote because of race or color.
The 16th Amendment:	gave Congress the right to create an income tax.
The 17th Amendment:	changed the way senators were chosen.
The 18th Amendment:	made it unlawful to make, sell, or transport liquor.
The 19th Amendment:	says that people cannot be denied the right to vote because of sex.
The 20th Amendment:	changed the day when the newly elected president could take office.
The 21st Amendment:	did away with the 18th Amendment.
The 22nd Amendment:	limits the number of terms a president can serve.
The 23rd Amendment:	gives a way for the citizens of the District of Columbia to vote for president.
The 24th Amendment:	did away with any taxes that had to be paid in order to vote.
The 25th Amendment:	says that the vice-president becomes president if the president is not able to continue in office.
The 26th Amendment:	gave 18 year olds the right to vote.

31. The Leaders of Congress

There are many important leaders in Congress. These leaders help Congress set up its daily activities. They work closely with the president on new laws.

All members of Congress belong to a political party. The two parties that most people belong to are the Republican and Democratic parties. The party with the most members represented in Congress is called the **majority party**. The party with fewer members is called the **minority party**.

Congress is set up around a two-party system. The majority party has the power to pass many laws. The leaders in Congress are usually members of the majority party. The leaders in Congress are able to get much support for new laws. This is because many times members of the majority party will team together to vote *yes* for a certain law.

Who are the leaders in Congress? Congress has seven important leaders. They are:

- Speaker of the House
- president of the Senate
- president pro tempore of the Senate
- majority party leader of each house
- minority party leader of each house.

What is the job of the Speaker of the House? The Speaker of the House is the presiding officer of the House of Representatives. The Speaker is elected by the members of the House. The Speaker receives $91,000 a year. Other members of Congress receive $69,800 a year.

The Speaker of the House has much power. These powers include:

- deciding which ideas for laws are discussed in the House.
- deciding which House member can speak on a bill.
- speeding up or slowing down the daily activities of the House.
- working directly with the president to get a law passed.
- being next in line for the presidency after the vice-president.

What do the majority and minority leaders do? Both the majority and minority party leaders help get ideas for new laws passed. They can also help stop new laws from being passed. Party members listen to these leaders closely.

There is a majority and minority party leader in each house of Congress. They are chosen by the members of their party. They must be good at helping Congress to set up its activities.

Who is the leader in the Senate? The vice-president is the leader of the Senate. When the vice-president presides over the Senate, he has a special title. Then the vice-president is called the president of the Senate.

The vice-president presides over all Senate meetings. The vice-president can only vote in the case of a tie. Also, he cannot talk about an idea for a new law while presiding over the Senate.

The Senate elects a president pro tempore (in place of) to preside over the Senate when the vice-president is not able to.

National Geographic Society photographer
courtesy U.S. Capitol Historical Society

Tip O'Neill meets with other Congressmen in his office.

32. The Committee System

Congress has much work to do. The members of Congress must talk about thousands of ideas for new laws. Only a few of these ideas for laws really become laws. Much of the work that Congress does is done in **committees.**

Why are committees needed? All ideas for new laws are written down. Sometimes it takes many pages to write about an idea. All the members of **Congress do not have time to read** about every idea for a new law. Committees are set up to review suggested or **proposed** new laws. The members of each committee read about the proposed new laws given to the committee they are on.

Also, members may become experts on one or two areas of government. They may know a lot about the country's land, or water, or health. In this case, the members are put on committees that talk about their special interests.

How are the committees set up? All ideas for new laws are divided into different groups. Each type of proposed law has a committee. There are 22 major committees in the House of Representatives. There are 15 major committees in the Senate.

Sometimes the committees have too much to do. When this happens a committee forms subcommittees. The subcommittees look into specific areas. They report back to the whole committee. The whole committee then reports to Congress.

What is the job of each committee? Each committee talks about the good and bad parts of a proposed new law. Sometimes, the ideas are rewritten, adding parts and taking parts out.

As part of their work, committees often hold hearings.

The committee may agree that a new law should be passed. In this case, the committee tells this to all the members of Congress. Congress then votes *yes* or *no* on the proposed new law. If both Houses of Congress vote *yes*, it becomes a law.

Do all members of Congress serve on a committee? Yes, all members of Congress are on at least one committee. Senators are usually on two committees. Representatives are usually on just one committee. Members may also be on more than one subcommittee.

Who decides which member should be on a committee? Membership of each committee is decided by many things. Some things that are considered are:

- the member's interest in a certain area of government.
- how long the person has been a member of Congress.
- how the leaders of Congress feel about the skills of the member.

The membership of some committees is chosen by a vote of the entire body. Members of other committees are appointed. They are appointed by the leaders of Congress.

Some committees are more important than others. The power to appoint members gives the leaders of Congress much control over certain committees.

33. The Different Committees of Congress

There are four different types of committees in Congress. These are:

- standing committees
- special committees
- joint committees
- conference committees.

As you know, the job of a committee is to look at new ideas for laws. Committees can also investigate areas of government. This looking into can cover many important topics.

For example, in 1974, a committee in the House of Representatives investigated President Richard Nixon. The committee was trying to decide if President Nixon should be impeached.

President Nixon left office before the committee finished its study.

Committees usually hold open meetings. This means that anyone can watch and listen to the committee meeting. Sometimes, a committee will close its meeting. This is only done in very special cases.

Are all committees made up of representatives and senators? No, only the joint and conference committees are made up of representatives and senators. Standing and special committees are made up of only members from one house of Congress. It works like this:

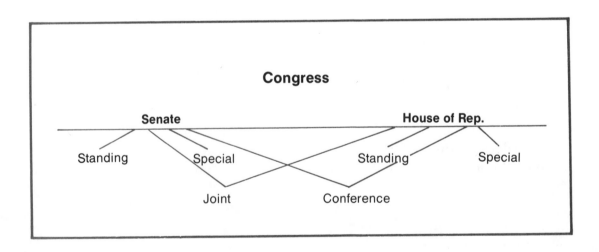

Congress

Senate   House of Rep.

Standing   Special   Standing   Special

Joint   Conference

Standing Committees of Congress

House of Representatives

Agriculture
Appropriations
Armed Services
Banking, Finance and Urban Affairs
Budget
District of Columbia
Education and Labor
Energy and Commerce
Foreign Affairs
Government Operations
House Administration
Interior and Insular Affairs
Judiciary
Merchant Marine and Fisheries
Post Office and Civil Service
Public Works and Transportation
Rules
Science and Technology
Small Business
Standards of Official Conduct
Veterans' Affairs
Ways and Means

Senate

Agriculture, Nutrition, and Forestry
Appropriations
Armed Services
Banking, Housing, and Urban Affairs
Budget
Commerce, Science, and Transportation
Energy and Natural Resources
Environment and Public Works
Finance
Foreign Relations
Governmental Affairs
Judiciary
Labor and Human Resources
Rules and Administration
Veterans' Affairs

What do standing committees do?
The standing committees are the major committees in Congress. Members are elected by a vote. All ideas for new laws are talked about in the standing committees. Standing committees also study areas of concern. They last from one session of Congress to another.

What are special committees?
Special committees are also called select committees. Special committees usually last for only one year. They are set up to look into a certain problem. Examples of special committees are the House's Select Committee on the Aging and the Senate's Select Committee on Indian Affairs.

What is the difference between joint and conference committees? Joint committees are made up of members from both houses of Congress. They are set up to look into certain areas of government.

Conference committees are also made up of senators and representatives. Sometimes an idea for a law cannot be agreed on by both houses of Congress. In this case, a conference committee will talk about the idea. The committee will then rewrite the idea in a new form which it thinks will then pass both houses.

34. Making a Law

Laws are made to help solve the nation's problems. Laws are also made to watch over the rights of people.

Laws affect everyone. The law says that everyone must pay taxes. The law says that adult citizens have the right to vote. The law also tells us what we can and cannot do. Laws help people know what is right and wrong.

Not everyone agrees with the laws of our country. Also, new problems often need new laws to help solve them. When this happens, Congress must make new laws.

As you already know, ideas for new laws are called bills. All bills are written. A bill can be presented in either the Senate or the House first. There is only one exception. All bills about raising money must begin in the House of Representatives.

Sometimes a bill is presented in both houses at the same time. Once a bill has been presented, it is given a number. Members of Congress use these numbers to refer to the bills.

Who gives members of Congress ideas for bills? Anyone can give a member of Congress a bill. Many bills come from the president. Other bills come from groups of people who would like to see a law changed or a new law made. Sometimes, a senator or representative may like to see a law changed or a new law made. The senator or representative then writes a bill.

Sometimes, committees may see the need for a new law. They may write a bill. This usually happens after an investigation.

Over 20,000 new bills are given to Congress every term. Only about 1,000 of these bills become laws.

What happens after a bill is presented in one of the houses? After a bill is presented in either the House or Senate, it is given to the proper standing committee.

The chairman of the standing committee then decides if the bill is good or not. If the chairman feels the bill is good, a hearing on it will be called. If the chairman feels the bill is not good, a hearing will not be called. If there is no hearing, it is almost certain that the bill will never become a law. The bill is said to have "died in committee."

If a hearing is called, many people will be asked to discuss the bill. This gives the committee members a chance to hear why people are for or against the proposed law.

What happens next? The standing committee may like the bill as written. Or it may rewrite the bill. If the committee approves the bill, it is reported out of committee to the rest of the house. Now it is ready to be discussed by the whole house.

The Rules Committee of each house decides when a bill will be discussed by the whole house. Bills that the Rules Committee feels are important are usually discussed first. This gives the Rules Committee much power over each bill.

Only bills which both the standing and Rules Committees approve are discussed by all members of a house.

In the House of Representatives there is a limit on how long a bill can be discussed. The majority and minority parties in the House are able to discuss a bill for the same amount of time. After the time is up, each representative votes either *yes* or *no* on the bill. If the majority votes *yes*, the bill is then sent to the Senate. If a bill passes both houses, it is then sent to the president.

Is there a time limit in the Senate? No, there is no time limit in the Senate.

A senator can talk for an unlimited amount of time on a bill. Sometimes if a senator does not like a bill, the senator will talk for hours. The senator does this to make the other senators so tired that they will vote against the bill. This kind of talking is known as a **filibuster.**

Senators must stand while talking in the Senate. As long as they stand, they can talk about anything. Stories can even be read.

Can a filibuster be stopped? Yes, a filibuster can be stopped. The Senate can use the **closure rule**. This means that the Senate takes a vote. If two-thirds of the senators vote to end the filibuster, then it stops. The closure rule is not used very often though.

What happens if one house likes a bill and the other house does not? If either house changes a part of a bill, the bill must go back to the first house for approval. Sometimes, both houses of Congress cannot agree on a bill. When this happens, a conference committee is set up to rewrite the bill. The bill is then rewritten so that both houses will approve the changes.

As you can see, there are many long steps before a bill becomes a law. If a bill is not approved by the end of one term of Congress, the bill dies. Even if the bill is approved by both houses, it still isn't a law. There is one more step before a bill becomes a law.

35. The President Acts on Bills

Before a bill can become a law many people must approve the bill. Even if Congress approves a bill, the president may not like it. It is the job of the president to take the final action on each bill that Congress approves.

After a bill is approved by Congress it is sent to the president. The president now has four choices. He may:

- sign the bill.
- do nothing.
- **pocket veto** the bill.
- veto the bill.

What happens if the president signs the bill? If the president signs the bill, the bill becomes a law. The president must like the whole bill. He cannot cross out parts or change the bill. Most bills are signed by the president.

What if the president does nothing about a bill? Sometimes, a president may not agree with a bill. However, the president may not disagree with it either. If the president does not want to take a stand on a bill, he can do

nothing. If the president does nothing, a bill will become a law in ten days. This will only happen if Congress stays in session for those ten days.

When the president pocket vetoes a bill, he does not really put it in his pocket. However, the effect is almost the same.

Members of Congress meet in the U.S. Capitol Building in Washington, D.C.

What is a pocket veto? Sometimes, Congress **adjourns**, takes a break, after a bill is sent to the president. The president may then choose to do nothing about the bill. When this happens the bill does *not* become a law. This is called a pocket veto. It is as though the president put the bill in a pocket, Congress went home, and everybody forgot about the bill.

What is the difference between a veto and a pocket veto? A veto is saying *no* to a bill. When the president vetoes a bill, a formal message is sent to Congress. In the message, the president tells why the bill was vetoed.

When the president pocket vetoes a bill, the president simply does no-

thing. Since Congress has adjourned, no message can be sent to Congress.

Sometimes, the president likes only part of a bill. The president vetoes the bill telling Congress what part was not liked. The bill is returned to Congress. If Congress can rewrite the bill, the president may then sign it.

Can Congress do anything if the president vetoes a bill? Yes, Congress can say *no* to the president's veto. This is called overriding the veto.

To override a veto, two-thirds of each house must vote to say *no* to the president's veto. When this happens, the bill becomes law even though the president has not signed it.

Making a Law

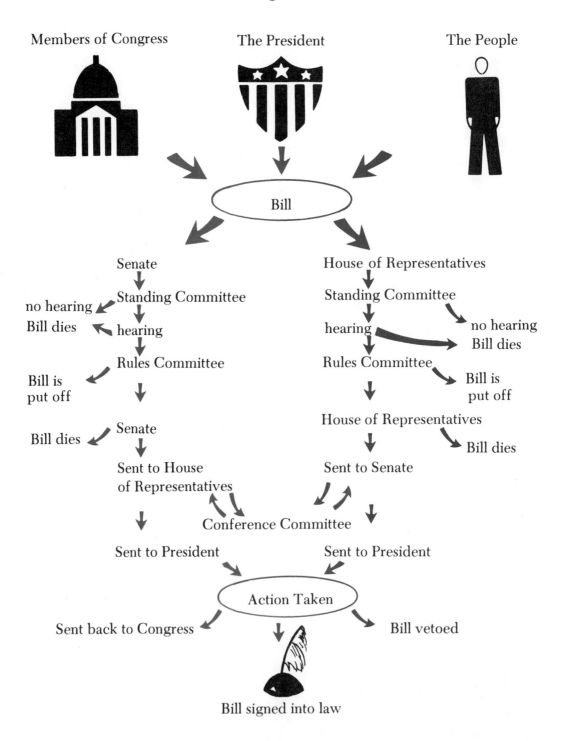

Members of Congress

The President

The People

Bill

Senate

Standing Committee

no hearing
Bill dies

hearing

Rules Committee

Bill is
put off

Bill dies

Senate

Sent to House
of Representatives

Sent to President

House of Representatives

Standing Committee

hearing

no hearing
Bill dies

Rules Committee

Bill is
put off

House of Representatives

Bill dies

Sent to Senate

Conference Committee

Sent to President

Action Taken

Sent back to Congress

Bill vetoed

Bill signed into law

Unit 4 Summary

The legislative branch of our government is also called Congress. Congress is made up of two houses called the Senate and the House of Representatives.

There are 535 members of Congress. 100 members are senators. 435 members are representatives. Every state has two senators. The number of representatives for each state depends on the number of people in the state.

Congress has many lawmaking powers. They are called expressed and implied powers. Congress also has four important non-lawmaking powers.

Most of the work of Congress is done in committees. The leaders of Congress help to organize the committees. All members of Congress are on committees.

An idea for a new law is called a bill. All bills are sent to a standing committee. The standing committees of each house report on the bill that they like. A bill must be approved by both houses of Congress.

The president can choose to sign a bill into law. Or the president can veto it. In certain cases a bill can become law even if the president does not sign it.

UNIT 5
The Judicial Branch

The purpose of the judicial branch is to explain the meaning of the laws Congress makes. The judicial branch also makes sure that all laws are fair. This is a very important job in our government.

The judicial branch is composed of the federal courts. This includes many courts throughout the country. It also includes the Supreme Court of the United States.

The Supreme Court is a very special court. It is the most powerful of all the federal courts. There is only one Supreme Court for the entire country. The Supreme Court has a special job. It explains the Constitution.

How is the judicial branch set up? What types of federal courts are there? How are laws reviewed by the courts? Unit 5 answers these and other questions.

By the end of this unit you should be able to:

- explain the purpose of the three major federal courts.
- list seven special courts.
- explain how a case gets to the Supreme Court.

New York Convention and Visitor's Bureau

36. The Supreme Court

The Supreme Court is the highest court in the United States. It has the most power. It first held court in 1790.

The Supreme Court is the only court set up by the Constitution. All other federal courts have been set up by Congress.

Who serves on the Supreme Court? There are nine **justices** that preside over the Supreme Court. A justice is a judge who presides over an important court. The country's most important court is the Supreme Court. So the judges who sit on this court are called justices.

Supreme Court Historical Society

Members of the Supreme Court. Top row from left to right: John P. Stevens; L.F. Powell, Jr.; W.H. Rehnquist; Sandra Day O'Connor. Seated from left to right: Thurgood Marshall; W.J. Brennan, Jr.; Chief Justice Warren E. Burger; Byron R. White; Harry A. Blackman.

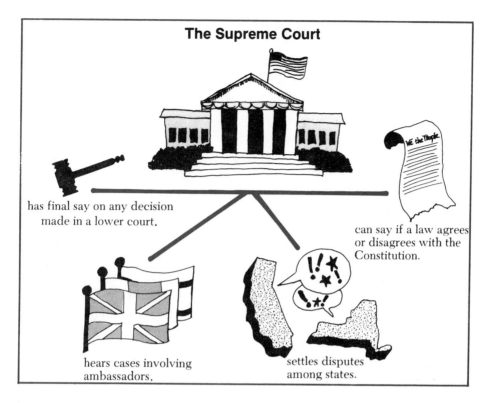

The Supreme Court

has final say on any decision made in a lower court.

can say if a law agrees or disagrees with the Constitution.

hears cases involving ambassadors.

settles disputes among states.

The president appoints each justice. They serve for life. This means the justices may remain on the court until retirement or death. However, a justice may be impeached by Congress for wrong-doing.

Why is the Supreme Court the most powerful court? The Supreme Court has the final say on all laws and the Constitution. Look at the chart above. It shows the many powers of the Supreme Court.

Is the Supreme Court ever the first to hear a case? Yes, the Supreme Court has **original jurisdiction** over two kinds of cases. This means that the Supreme Court is the first court to hear these cases. Because the Supreme Court is the highest court in the land, it is also the only court to hear them. These cases are:

- cases about disagreements between two or more states.
- cases about ambassadors.

Most other cases reach the Supreme Court by **appeal.**

What is an appeal? To appeal a case means to ask a higher court to review a decision made by a lower court. People who are unhappy with a court decision often ask for appeals. However, appeals are only granted for a reason. The higher court will look at the information about a case. Then it will decide if there's a good reason why the lower court's decision should be changed. Sometimes, it will decide that there should be a whole new trial. But this is rare.

37. Supreme Court Decisions

All Supreme Court decisions are important. They affect everyone. But some cases stand out as being **landmark** cases. That is, they are especially important. These cases have made major changes in our country.

How are decisions made? The Supreme Court is in session from October to June. Each month is divided into two parts. For the first two weeks, justices hear lawyers talk about their cases. For the next two weeks, the justices meet. At this time, they make decisions about the cases. About 4,200 decisions are made each term.

The justices vote for or against a case. Cases are decided by a majority vote. A majority vote is one vote more than half. On the Supreme Court, a majority vote is five justices.

This 1861 engraving shows slaves being offered for sale. Before the Civil War, slavery was practiced in some states.

After voting, a majority **opinion** is written. This is a statement explaining the decision.

Any justice voting against the majority may write a minority opinion. This statement explains why the justice disagreed with the majority's decision. Opinions are read in court.

What was an important Supreme Court decision? One very important Supreme Court decision was the Dred Scott v. Sandford case. It happened in 1857.

Dred Scott was a black. He had been born a slave. Then he moved with his owner to Illinois. Illinois did not permit slavery. Dred Scott said that he should be free.

The Supreme Court said a black man had no rights. Dred Scott had to remain a slave. The Dred Scott decision caused many bad feelings. This further divided the people who were for or against slavery.

What was another important case in the Supreme Court? Plessy v. Ferguson (1896) was an important decision. In this case, the Supreme Court said that it was all right for blacks and whites to have separate railway cars. However, the cars had to be the same. This Supreme Court decision set the "separate but equal" idea. This meant that separation of the races was legal as long as the places were the same.

Is "separate but equal" still lawful today? No, "separate but equal" is not lawful today. The case, Brown v. Board of Education, changed this idea in 1954.

This case began in Topeka, Kansas. The Supreme Court decided that schools could not keep black children from going to school with white children. Separate schools for whites and blacks were no longer equal. This decision changed the "separate but equal" idea.

As you can see, the Supreme Court has changed its decisions over time. This is because new justices with new ideas have presided over the court. They have looked at the Constitution in different ways.

All children have the right to be educated. Above, students are involved in a summer reading program.

38. The United States District Courts

The United States district courts were set up by Congress in 1789. The 13 district courts were spread throughout the new country. The district courts were given original jurisdiction over cases about federal law. Thus, in the early years of our federal court system, we had only two types of courts. These were the Supreme Court and the district courts.

Does this mean that federal cases start in district courts? Yes, most federal cases do start in district courts. Only cases between state governments or ambassadors do not start in district courts.

What is a federal case? A federal case is about a federal law. A person who might have broken a federal law is brought to trial in a district court.

There are two kinds of cases brought to district courts. These are called **criminal** and **civil** cases. A criminal case involves a federal law being broken. A civil case involves a disagreement between people. An example is when one person sues another.

Another kind of civil case heard in federal court involves a person's rights being denied. For example, this may be over not being able to speak or worship freely. Our rights are stated in the Constitution and its amendments. They may not be denied. If they are denied, the case can be taken to federal court.

Are federal cases heard by only one judge? In most district courts, only one judge presides. However, a **jury** is used in district courts. A jury is a group of people who listen to the case along with a judge. The jury helps the federal judge to make a decision about the case.

How are district courts set up? There are 94 U.S. district courts. These courts are spread throughout the country and its territories. Each state has at least one district court. Some states with more people have more than one district court. There are also district courts in Puerto Rico, Guam, the Virgin Islands, the Canal Zone, and one in the District of Columbia.

What happens if a person is not happy with a decision reached in a district court? People who are displeased with a decision reached in a U.S. district court can appeal it. Appeals are made to a U.S. court of appeals.

Can a state court appeal a decision to a U.S. district court? Most cases about a state law can only be heard by a state court. A case about a state law which may not agree with a federal law may be heard in a U.S. district court. All state laws must agree with federal laws.

UPI/Bettmann Archive

Supporters of Rev. Sun Myung Moon rally outside a U.S. district court in New York City. Rev. Moon was accused and later found guilty of filing false income tax returns.

39. The United States Courts of Appeals

Word to know
circuit

United States courts of appeals are also called **circuit** courts. In the early days of our federal court system, Supreme Court justices traveled certain regions, called circuits, on horseback. In this way, the judicial needs of the country were taken care of.

In 1891, Congress set up nine circuit courts of appeals. In 1948, the circuit courts of appeals changed their name to courts of appeals.

What is the purpose of the United States courts of appeals? The U.S. courts of appeals only hear cases that are appealed to them from the district courts. They do not hear a complete trial. Their purpose is to review the decision of the district court. Three justices usually hear each case.

A decision reached by a U.S. district court may be changed or agreed with in a U.S. court of appeals. Sometimes the court may send the case back to the district court for another trial.

What happens if a person is not happy with a decision reached in a U.S. court of appeals? Some people are not happy with the decision reached in a U.S. court of appeals. A decision that is not agreed with can be appealed to the Supreme Court.

Not all cases appealed to the Supreme Court will be heard by the

U.S. Courts of Appeals

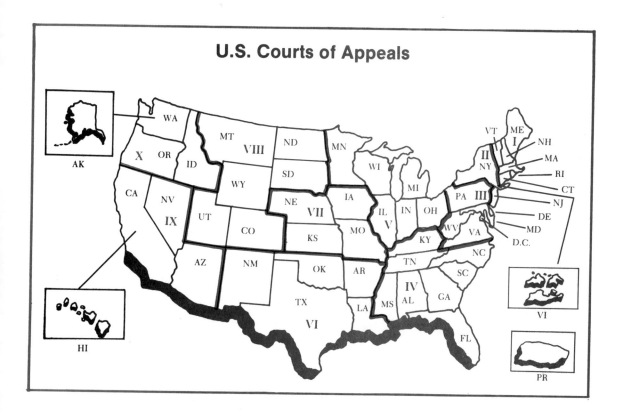

Supreme Court. Many times, the Supreme Court agrees with the decision reached in a U.S. court of appeals.

How many U.S. courts of appeals are there? The United States is divided into 11 regions or circuits. Each circuit has one U.S. court of appeals. There is also one U.S. court of appeals in the District of Columbia (Washington, D.C.). So there are really 12 U.S. courts of appeals in all.

Look at the map above. Find the state in which you live. What circuit court are you in?

40. The Special Federal Courts

There are also special courts. These courts have been set up by Congress. The courts were set up to hear special kinds of cases.

Can a court hear a case against the government? In 1855, the U.S. Court of Claims was set up. It was set up for anyone who had a money claim against the government. A claim against the government must be made within six years.

Claims against the government could include such things as collecting back pay, or seeking land that the government took away.

Are there ever cases about taxes? Cases over how much tax a person should pay are heard in tax court. The U.S. Tax Court was set up in 1924.

Sometimes a person disagrees with how much taxes the government says

must be paid. These tax disagreements are settled in tax court.

The U.S. Customs Court hears cases on special taxes, called **customs**, paid on goods brought into the country. This court was set up in 1926.

The Court of Customs and Patent Appeals was set up in 1907. It hears appeals on customs and **patent** cases. A patent is a legal document that protects the rights of an inventor. Cases heard in this court could include:

- a case lost in customs court.
- a case where someone was not given a patent on an invention.
- a case about someone bringing goods into the country against the law.

Are there other kinds of federal courts? Yes, there are several. The Court of Military Appeals was set up in 1950. It hears appeals from persons

Customs agents often use specially trained dogs to search for illegal items coming into the country.

in the army and navy who have been convicted of a crime. Decisions made by the Court of Military Appeals are final. No further appeals to any other federal court can be made.

Also, there are four territorial courts. They are in Guam, the Virgin Islands, the Panama Canal, and Puerto Rico. A territory is a country governed by the United Sates. A territory is not a state, however.

The territorial courts act as district courts in these countries. Appeals from the territorial courts can be made to a U.S. court of appeals.

Are there courts in the District of Columbia? Yes, there are many courts in the District of Columbia. This is because it has special local jurisdiction.

The main court in the District of Columbia is a U.S. district court. There is also a U.S. court of appeals. The District of Columbia has many less powerful courts, too. These include a court for those people under 17, a small claims court, and a city court.

41. The Federal Judges

The judges serving on the federal courts have a very important job. They must make sure that all laws are fair. They also make sure that all laws agree with the United States Constitution.

How are federal judges chosen? Federal judges who serve on federal courts are chosen by the president. The president usually chooses a person from his political party. All federal judges appointed by the president must be approved by a two-thirds vote of the Senate. Federal judges are not elected by the people.

How long are federal judges in office? A federal judge stays in office for a life term. No judge can be removed from office for poor health.

A federal judge may retire from office. Federal judges may also be forced to leave office through impeach-

Sandra Day O'Conner appears to check her robe as she waits to take her oath of office. She is the 102nd justice of the Supreme Court and the 1st female Supreme Court justice.

UPI/Bettmann Archive

ment. For this to happen the House of Representatives would have to impeach a federal judge. The Senate would then hold a trial. Only four judges have been impeached throughout history.

Does a federal judge also have to be a lawyer? No, federal judges do not have to be lawyers. However, so far all federal judges have been lawyers.

How old must a person be to be a federal judge? The Constitution sets no age limit for federal judges. In fact, the Constitution sets no special qualifications for federal judges. But federal judges are appointed with care. People with very good skills in law are most often chosen.

How much are federal judges paid? The highest paid federal judge is the chief justice of the Supreme Court. This person makes $96,800 per year. The other eight Supreme Court justices make $93,000 per year. District and court of appeals justices make less than Supreme Court justices.

What special duties do federal judges have? A federal judge's job is demanding. Much work needs to be done. Federal judges have a staff of lawyers and clerks to help them do their job well.

Federal judges have some very important duties. These include:

- deciding what information about a case can be brought into court.
- running a trial.
- studying what is written about a case.
- making sure everyone in court is treated fairly.
- deciding how someone should be punished for committing a crime.
- checking on whether any old laws apply to a case.
- giving directions to the jury.
- making sure that everyone behaves properly in court.

Judicial Branch

```
                    ┌─────────────────────────────────────┐
                    │                                     │
                    │  Supreme Court of the United States │
                    │                                     │
                    └─────────────────────────────────────┘
```

United States district courts 94 districts in the 50 states, the District of Columbia, Puerto Rico, Guam, the Virgin Islands, and the Canal Zone	United States courts of appeals 12 circuits in the 50 states and the District of Columbia	Special courts (Various courts created by Congress to hear certain cases)
		1. Court of Claims 2. Customs court 3. Court of Customs and Patent Appeals 4. Tax court 5. Court of Military Appeals 6. Territorial courts

Unit 5 Summary

The federal court system is called the judicial branch of our government. There are three main court systems in the federal court system. There is the U.S. Supreme Court, the U.S. courts of appeals, and the U.S. district courts. There are also seven special courts to hear cases on special matters.

Both criminal and civil cases can be heard in federal court. All civil cases must be for suits of over $10,000.

All federal justices are appointed by the president. They may preside over a court for a life term. Congress can impeach a justice and the justice may be removed from court.

People who are not happy with a decision reached in a federal court can appeal the decision to a higher federal court. The Supreme Court has the final say in all appeals. It is the highest court in the land.

UNIT 6
Checks and Balances

As you have learned, the three branches of government have many important duties. They share many powers. However, our three branches of government also watch over each other. This watching over is known as checks and balances. Each branch acts as a check (a control) on the other two branches. The three branches also balance each other's powers. That way no single branch becomes too powerful. The system of checks and balances was set up by the Constitution.

There is another way that the power of government as a whole is checked. This way is not mentioned in the Constitution. It has come about because we are a democracy. People help to check the power of government. They can do this in several ways.

How does each branch check the other branches? What are the balances of power in our government? How can people check the power of government? You will learn the answers to all these questions in Unit 6.

By the end of this unit you should be able to:

- list three checks for each branch.
- tell why checks and balances are important.
- explain how people can check the power of government.

Robert Bowie/Photo-Proof

42. The Purpose of the Checks and Balances System

Word to know
income

The writers of the Constitution wanted to make sure that the powers of the government would be shared. They did not want one branch of government to be more powerful than the other branches. They also did not want a strong executive power. They wanted all the people to have a say in government.

How does the Constitution make sure that one branch doesn't become too powerful? The Constitution calls for a separation, or division, of powers in our government. There are three main parts to the separation of powers idea:

- No person may serve in more than one branch at a time.
- The Constitution lists the powers and duties of each branch of government.
- Each branch has enough power to check the power of the other branches.

Separation of powers keeps one branch of government from becoming too powerful. It also gives many people a say in our government.

The system of checks and balances is a major part of the separation of powers idea. Because of our checks and balances system, one branch cannot work alone. All three branches must work together. Each branch can check (control or stop) what another branch is doing. Each branch can also balance the powers of another branch by working together.

Has the system of checks and balances been used often? Yes, the system of checks and balances is used often. Many changes in our government have come from the use of checks and balances.

The 16th Amendment is an example of how checks and balances have changed our government. In 1895, Congress passed the income tax laws. This law gave the federal government the right to tax citizens' incomes. (**Income** is the money someone receives such as wages.)

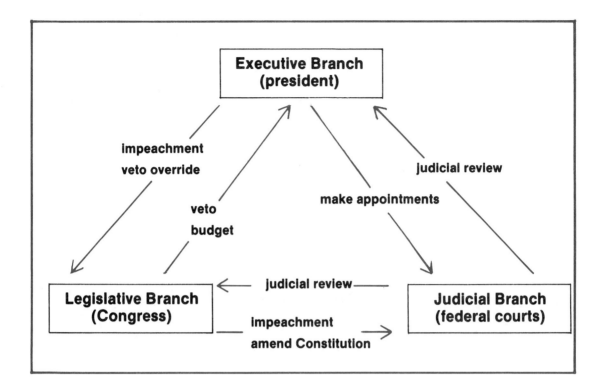

The Supreme Court ruled that an income tax did not agree with the Constitution. But Congress and the president did not agree with this decision. They felt an income tax was needed. Congress then passed the 16th Amendment in 1913. This amendment gives Congress the right to create an income tax.

What is another important example of how the checks and balances system works? Another example of how the checks and balances system works was in the 1930's. President Roosevelt wanted to make many changes. He wanted to start many new programs for the country. The Supreme Court disagreed with his ideas. President Roosevelt then tried to increase the number of justices on the Supreme Court.

This way he would be the one to choose the new justices. He planned on choosing justices who thought like he did. He thought this would help him get his programs started. But Congress would not allow President Roosevelt's Supreme Court idea to pass.

43. The Checking Power of the President

The president is our country's chief executive, chief legislator, chief diplomat, commander-in-chief, and chief jurist. These duties give the president some special checking powers. These checking powers give the president some control over the legislative and judicial branches.

How does the president check the legislative branch? The veto is the president's main check on the legislative branch. Sometimes the president does not like a bill for a new law. As you have already learned, the president can veto the bill. Vetoes are hard for Congress to override.

Is the veto used very often? Some presidents have made great use of their veto power. President Roosevelt vetoed 635 bills that Congress wrote. President Kennedy vetoed only 21 bills. President Nixon used his veto power 40 times.

Besides the veto, what other checks does the president have on Congress? The president has the right to call Congress into a special session. This is done whenever the president feels a very important law must be passed.

The president can also refuse to spend money on a program Congress wants. This power, however, is not given to the president by the Constitution. In fact, in 1975, the Supreme Court ruled that President Nixon did not have the power to **impound** funds for a New York City project.

The president also has the power to suggest new laws to Congress. Congress gives much thought and time to the president's ideas for new laws.

Are there some unwritten checks the president uses? Yes, the president has some very powerful unwritten checks. These include:

- speaking directly to the people for support of a new law.
- campaigning for the re-election of certain members of Congress.
- speaking as the head of a political party.

These unwritten checks are important to the president. The president can use them to **influence** or persuade Congress to pass laws that the president wants.

People all over the country watch and listen to the president. This gives the president a great deal of influence over Congress. The president is also regarded as the head of a political party. This gives the president much influence over members of Congress who belong to the same political party as the president.

How does the president check the judicial branch? All federal judges are appointed by the president. These include judges from the district courts to the Supreme Court.

The president tries to appoint a judge who will agree with him on many things. In this way, the president can influence the federal courts.

The president's power to appoint Supreme Court justices is an especially important power. It may give the president some influence over the court's decisions. But, not every president has the chance to appoint a Supreme Court justice. This is because justices serve for life. A president's term of office is only four years. So most presidents serve with a Supreme Court that other presidents have appointed.

Does the president have any checks against the actions of the federal courts? The president can grant a pardon to someone convicted of a federal crime. This does not include anyone convicted of impeachment. A person granted a pardon by the president is not punished for a crime.

Does the president have any other checks? Yes, one other check the president has is the budget. Remember, it is the president who puts together the country's budget. This affects everything in government. The president decides how much money should be spent by government. This is a very important power that the president can use to check the other branches. (But this power can also be checked by Congress. Congress must approve the president's budget.)

44. The Checking Power of Congress

Words to know	
acquitted	salaries

Congress also has the power of checks and balances. It can check both the executive and judicial branches.

How does Congress check the president? Congress has many checks over the executive branch. These include the power to:

- override the president's veto.
- approve all federal appointments made by the president.
- approve treaties the president makes with other countries.
- approve the president's budget.
- impeach a federal official, including the president.

Was a president ever impeached? In 1868, the House of Representatives voted to impeach President Andrew Jackson. The Senate later **acquitted** President Jackson. To acquit means to free from the charges. The vote was close for President Jackson. If one more senator had voted yes, he would have been removed from office.

In 1974, over 100 years later, the House of Representatives was again deciding if the president should be impeached. This time the president was President Richard Nixon. President Nixon left office. He did not want to test the House's impeachment powers. Later, President Ford pardoned President Nixon. President Ford could do this because President Nixon was never impeached.

How does the House impeach a federal official? A committee of the House of Representatives holds hearings. Then the committee reports its findings to the whole House. The House of Representatives then votes on the impeachment.

A federal official impeached by the House of Representatives stands trial in the Senate. The Senate sits as the jury. The Senate may vote to remove the official from office. It takes a two-thirds majority to do this.

A federal official removed from office may be tried in federal court. The trial is about any crimes committed while in office.

What checks does Congress have over the judicial branch? Congress must approve all federal judge appointments. Congress also has the power to impeach a federal judge. So far, the House of Representatives has voted to impeach nine federal judges. Four of these men were removed from office by the Senate. The last time this happened was in 1936.

Are most federal judges appointed to office approved of by the Senate? All appointments of federal judges are looked at closely by Congress. Most are approved. Once in a while, federal judge appointments run into trouble. President Nixon, for example, had two Supreme Court appointments turned down by the Senate.

Can Congress change the number of federal judges? Yes, Congress has the power to change the number of federal judges. Congress also has the power to decide on the **salaries** of federal judges. A salary is the amount of money someone is paid to do a job.

What happens if the Supreme Court says a law does not agree with the Constitution? In this case, Congress can try to amend the Constitution. Remember, this happened with the 16th Amendment. Amending the Constitution does not happen very often though.

Congress acts as the people's representative to check the other two branches of government. Above, members of the Senate are gathered.

45. The Checking Power of the Judicial Branch

The checking power of the judicial branch is called **judicial review.** Judicial review means looking closely to see if laws are fair to everyone. The judicial branch has the power of judicial review over both the legislative and executive branches.

How does judicial review apply to the president? The court can review the president's actions. It can decide if the president is doing something that is unconstitutional. That is, it can decide if something does not agree with the Constitution.

What power does the federal court have over the president? A federal court can limit the actions of the president. The federal courts can stop what the president plans to do. A federal court can also force the president to do something. This is called placing an **injunction** on the president's actions.

What is another power the federal court has over the president? Another power the federal court has over the president is judicial review. A good example of how judicial review over the president was used is Watergate.

Watergate began in June, 1972. At this time, five men were caught illegally entering the sixth floor of the Watergate Hotel. The Democratic party had its main office on the sixth floor. During this time, President Nixon was campaigning to be elected again as president. He was a Republican. Some people said that the men caught at the Watergate Hotel were trying to get secret information. They said that this information would help President Nixon to get re-elected. Not many people believed these charges.

President Nixon was re-elected in November, 1972. In January, 1973, the nation was surprised with some news about Watergate. One of the men caught entering the Watergate Hotel said that people in the White House knew about the break-in. Many men on President Nixon's staff were charged with knowing about it. President Nixon denied knowing anything about the Watergate break-in before it happened.

Later, it was found out that President Nixon had secret tapes. These tapes were on talks he had with his staff. It was thought that the tapes would have some information about the Watergate break-in.

The Senate asked President Nixon to give up the tapes. President Nixon said *no*. He said that he did not have to give the tapes to the Senate because he was the president. The Senate went to court to get the tapes.

Judge Sirica, a federal court judge, said that the president must give up the tapes. Finally, the President Nixon appealed to the Supreme Court. The president said that the Senate did not have the right to go to court against the president. The Supreme Court disagreed with President Nixon. President Nixon was ordered to give up the tapes. Later, President Nixon left office. He was the first president to ever do this.

What judicial review power is there over the Congress? Any federal court can say that a law passed by Congress does not agree with the Constitution. Once a federal court says this, the law cannot be used any longer.

Do federal courts have any judicial review power over state laws? Yes, federal courts have judicial review powers over state laws. All state laws must agree with federal laws and the Constitution. Federal courts can decide if the laws do agree.

UPI/Bettmann Archive

Judge John J. Sirica was the trial judge in the Watergate bugging case.

46. The People's Checking Power

<table>
<tr><td>Words to know

interest groups   unions
lobbying</td></tr>
</table>

In a democracy, people act as another way to check and balance the powers of government as a whole.

How can people check the power of government? The most obvious way people can check the power of government is by voting. It is the people who elect the members of government. Members of government should respond to the needs of the people they represent. It is up to the people to let their representatives know what they need. The people must also let their representatives know if they are unhappy with them. One way of doing this is through the vote.

Are there any other ways to influence government? Yes, there are other ways to influence government. Sometimes, people who feel very strongly about a certain issue will join together. They will form a group. Such groups are called **interest groups.**

Who belongs to interest groups? Many people belong to interest groups. Sometimes, the people in a neighborhood may get together because of a common complaint. They may try to put pressure on city leaders to change a city law. Putting pressure on government leaders is called **lobbying.**

Interest groups and lobbying form an important part of our political process. That is, they are not a formal part of our government, but they have a strong influence on its decisions.

Who else forms interest groups? There are also some highly organized interest groups. These groups may be very large. They may have members from all across the country. Some of these interest groups are made up of workers. Some are called **unions.** An example of an interest group made up of workers is the AFL-CIO (American Federation of Labor and Congress of Industrial Organizations). Unions like the AFL-CIO lobby for laws that favor workers. Businesses also belong to interest groups. These groups want laws that favor business.

Some interest groups serve to protect the interests of a particular race, sex, or religious group. An example is NOW (the National Organization for Women). Currently, NOW is lobbying for passage of the ERA.

Interest groups are one more way people can become involved in government. They are also another way that the power of government is divided and separated.

Unit 6 Summary

Our government has three branches. Each branch works to check the power of the other two. This is known as the system of checks and balances. It was set up by the Constitution.

The president is able to check Congress. The president may veto bills that Congress wants to become laws. The president may also call Congress into a special session. The president may also refuse to spend money on programs Congress wants.

The president checks the judicial branch by being able to appoint federal judges and justices. The president can also grant pardons in federal cases.

Congress is able to check the president. It can override the president's veto. It must also approve many of the president's actions. Congress also has the power of impeachment over all federal officials.

Congress is able to check the judicial branch. It must approve all federal judge appointments. Congress can also amend the Constitution.

The judicial branch has the power of judicial review over both the executive and legislative branches. It can also review state laws to see if they agree with federal laws.

People can also check the powers of government. They can do this by voting. They can also do this by joining interest groups and lobbying.

UNIT 7

State Government

The Constitution divided power among federal and state governments. This is called federalism. You have learned about our country's federal Constitution and government. Now you are going to learn about state government. And you know what? States also have constitutions.

A state's constitution is very important. It is the plan for the state's government. The State constitution may also contain plans for local government. The rights of the people are listed in the state constitution. Every state constitution says that government belongs to the people.

The constitution of every state divides the government into three branches. The three branches are the executive, legislative, and judicial branches. As you can see, the plan for federal and state governments is the same.

What are the powers of the governor? How are the federal and state legislative branches the same? What types of courts do the states have? How are the federal and state governments the same? How are they different? You will learn the answers to all these questions in Unit 7.

By the end of Unit 7 you should be able to:

- compare the powers of the president with the powers of a governor.
- explain how state legislatures are set up.
- list three ways state and federal courts are the same.

47. The Governor

The head of the state executive branch is the governor. Each state has its own governor. The governor is elected by the people of the state. The governor's job is to make sure the laws of the state are obeyed. The governor may also give ideas for laws to the legislative branch. In some states, the governor appoints judges to the state's courts.

What decides the state powers of the governor? The state's constitution decides what the powers of the governor are. Thus, the governor's powers may differ from state to state. All governors have the same basic powers though. These include executive, legislative, and judicial powers.

What are the executive powers of the governor? The main executive power is to make sure the state's laws are obeyed. The governor may also appoint the heads of some executive departments. This power differs from state to state. In some states, the governor puts together the state's budget. The governor is also the commander-in-chief of the state's National Guard.

Another power many governors have is to make a **temporary** appoint-ment to the United States Senate. A governor could appoint someone to take the place of a senator until a new election could be held. This would only happen if a senator resigned or died while in office.

What are the legislative powers of a governor? The governor can give ideas for bills to the state legislature. The governor may also call special sessions of the legislature. Most governors have the power to veto bills. In many states the governor can veto parts of a bill. Remember, the president can only veto an entire bill.

What are the judicial powers of the governor? Many governors can appoint judges to state courts. Many governors may reduce a prisoner's sentence. Some governors may grant pardons. Some governors may order a prisoner set free.

How long is a governor's term in office? A governor's term can be for two or four years. The governor's salary also differs from state to state. For example, the governor of Massachusetts earns $40,000. The governor of Oregon earns $55,000. The governor of New Jersey earns $85,000.

48. Other State Officials

There are many other elected officials in the executive branch. They help the governor to carry out the laws of the state. These officials may or may not belong to the same political party as the governor.

What are some of the other officials in the executive branch? The lieutenant governor is one important official in the executive branch. The lieutenant governor takes the governor's place when the governor is absent, resigns, or dies.

Another important official is the Secretary of State. The Secretary of State keeps the official records of the state. This official also **publishes** (prints) the state's laws and watches over the state's elections.

States also have attorney generals. The Attorney General is the chief law officer of the state. The Attorney General represents the state in court and advises the governor on the state's laws.

Are there any other officials in the executive department? Yes, there are other officials in the executive department. Two are the treasurer and the comptroller.

The treasurer pays the state's bills. The treasurer also takes care of the state's money.

The comptroller keeps a record of all money taken in or paid out of the state treasury. In some states, the comptroller is called an auditor.

Do state governments also have executive departments? Yes, state governments also have many executive departments. These departments may deal with schools, roads, social services, or the environment. Many states also regulate certain businesses such as banking.

As you can see, the executive branch of state governments is very much like the executive branch of the federal government.

49. State Legislatures

Word to know

assembly

Each state has a legislative branch of government. Remember, the legislative branch makes the laws. In most states, the legislative branch is called the legislature. In some states, it is called the legislative **assembly.** In other states, it is called the general assembly. An assembly is a group of people who come together for a purpose. The purpose of the legislative assembly is to make laws.

How are state legislatures set up? Most state legislatures are divided into two houses. Nebraska has only one house. The upper house is called the Senate. The lower house is called the House of Representatives. In some states, the lower house is called the Assembly. It may also be called the House of Delegates. Members of the upper house are called senators. Members of the lower house are called representatives. In some states, members of the lower house are called members of the assembly.

How many state senators and representatives are there? This is decided by the number of districts in the state. Each state is divided into voting districts. Each district must have close to the same population. That is, each district must have about the same number of people. Larger districts are set up for electing senators. The state is also divided into smaller districts for electing representatives.

The size of the state legislature is different for each state. Virginia, for example, has 40 senators but only 80 members of the Assembly. The state of Rhode Island has 50 senators and 100 members of the Assembly.

How long is a session of the state legislature? Legislative sessions are different for each state. Some states meet for 60 to 90 days a year. Other states meet longer. Most sessions begin in January. The governor can also call special sessions. Here are some examples of legislative sessions:

Alaska meets every January for as long as necessary.

Minnesota meets for 120 days within two years.

Utah meets for 60 days beginning on the second Monday in January in odd-numbered years; meets for two days in even-numbered years.

State	Members of state legislature:
Alabama	receive $400 per month plus $67 per day in session.
Delaware	receive $12,198 per year.
Indiana	receive $9,600 per year plus $50 per day while in session and $12.50 per day when not is session.
Michigan	receive $31,000 per year plus $6,200 for expenses.
Ohio	receive $22,500 per year.
Vermont	receive $250 weekly while in session with a limit of $7,500 plus $50 per day while in special session.
Wisconsin	receive $22,638 per year plus $30 per day for expenses.
Wyoming	receive $30 per day while in session plus $60 per day for expenses.

What are the qualifications for a state senator? Each state sets its own qualifications for the elected officials of the state. This is decided by each state constitution. Members of the lower house usually must be at least 21 years old. Senators must usually be at least 25 years old.

Most states say that the representative or senator must live in his or her district. Some states say that members of the legislature must live in the state for a certain number of years.

How much do members of state legislatures earn? Members of state legislatures may serve for two or four years. This is decided on by the state. The salary of members of the legislature is also decided on by each state.

Most members of the lower house and senators earn a yearly salary.

The salaries are very different from state to state. In some states, extra money per day is given when the legislature meets. Some states also give money for traveling expenses. Look at the chart above. It gives some examples.

Do members of a state legislature work in committees like the members of Congress? Yes, members of state legislatures also work in committees. Most of the work of the state legislature is done in committees. Many of these committees meet all year long. State legislatures have standing committees and subcommittees. Special committees may be used. Joint committees may also be used. Remember, joint committees have members from both houses.

50. How a State Law Is Made

```
+---------------------------------+
|          Word to know           |
|           item veto             |
+---------------------------------+
```

State laws are made much the same way federal laws are made. It all begins with a member of the legislature writing a bill. Remember, a bill is the written idea for a new law. The ideas for bills can come from anyone.

What happens to a bill after it is written? After a bill is written, it goes to a committee. The committee discusses the bill. If the committee likes the bill then the whole house discusses and votes on it. If a majority in the house likes it, then it passes. Then it is sent to the other house. (If, that is, the state has two houses in its legislature. If it has only one, then the bill is sent directly to the governor.)

Once the bill is in the other house, the whole process repeats. If the bill passes the second house, it is sent to the governor.

Does the governor always sign bills? No, the governor does not always sign bills. The governor has veto power over bills. In many states a governor has a special veto power. It is called an **item veto.**

What is an item veto? Using an item veto, the governor can pass the parts of a bill. The governor vetoes only the parts not liked.

Can the state legislature override a governor's veto? Yes, state legislatures can override a governor's veto.

Do state laws sometimes become federal laws? Yes, there have been times when a state law has become a federal law. When this happens, many states may have to change their laws to agree with federal law. This is because all state laws must agree with federal laws.

An example of a state law becoming a federal law is the 18 year old vote. Some states had lowered their voting age to 18. Then in 1971, the 26th Amendment gave 18 year old citizens the right to vote. Other examples of this happening are the 15th and 19th Amendments.

The 15th Amendment says that no citizen may be denied the right to vote because of his or her race.

The 19th Amendment says that no citizen may be denied the right to vote because of sex. Thus, women were given the right to vote under the 19th Amendment.

Making a State Law

A member of the state legislature writes a bill. One house will debate it first.

A committee studies it. If it's passed, then the whole house discusses it.

or → It may die in committee.

If it passes in the house by a majority vote, it is sent to the other house.

or → It does not pass house vote.

A new committee studies it. If it's passed, the whole house discusses it.

or → It may die in committee.

The house votes and passes the bill.

or → It does not pass.

The governor signs the bill into law.

or → The governor vetoes the bill.

51. State Courts

The judicial branch is made up of many courts. Two kinds of cases are heard. These are criminal and civil cases. You have already learned that a civil case is a **dispute** (disagreement) between people. A divorce is an example of a civil case. A criminal case is when a criminal law is broken. Armed robbery is an example of a criminal case.

What are some of these courts? They include justice of the peace courts, police courts, city courts, and other special courts. They handle marriages, traffic tickets, small claims, and local laws.

General trial courts hear both civil and criminal cases. Cases are heard by a judge and jury. These courts can hear appeals from lower courts.

Appeals courts hear cases that are lost in lower courts. Appeals court judges study the trial. They decide if the **judgement** (decision) should be kept or changed. In some states, this is called the State Supreme Court. The State Supreme Court is the highest court for appealing cases about local or state law.

In some cases, an appeal is made to the United States Supreme Court. This only happens when a state law may not agree with a federal law.

Is a state judge appointed or elected? In some states, judges are elected by the people. In other states, judges are appointed by the governor. Most state judges have a term of 4 to 15 years, depending on the state.

In many states, a judge may be impeached. In others, a judge may be **recalled**. This is done by a recall election. In a recall election, the people vote for or against the judge. The judge is removed from office if the majority of people vote against the judge.

Unit 7 Summary

State government is very much like the federal government. It, too, has three branches.

The governor is the head of the executive branch. The governor makes sure the state's laws are obeyed. The governor can give ideas for bills. Many governors have the special power to item veto a bill. Governors also have judicial powers. In some states, this includes appointing judges. It may also include granting pardons.

The legislative branch of state government is called the state legislature or general assembly. Most state legislatures are divided into two houses. Members of state legislatures are elected.

Most of the legislature's work is done by committees. The committees study bills. A bill has to be approved by both houses. The governor may sign a bill into law. Or the governor may veto a bill.

The judicial branch is made up of state and local courts. The highest state court is the State Supreme Court. Sometimes, a case may be appealed to the United States Supreme Court. This happens when a state law may not agree with a federal law.

The three branches of state government check and balance each other. This way, no single branch can become too powerful.

UNIT 8

State Services

Americans have come to expect government to provide certain services. These include such things as education, roads, transportation, social services, and environmental programs.

Some of the money for these programs comes from the federal government. The federal government gives money to the states for many things. It is up to the states to see that this money is spent in the right way.

But the money states receive from the federal government isn't enough. States have to raise their own money, too. Each state decides how to raise money for its state services. Each state has much to say on how the money is spent.

What type of services does your state provide? Which services should be improved? Which services are more important than others? Where does a state get its money from? The answers to all these questions are in Unit 8.

By the end of this unit you should be able to:

- list five state services.
- list three things most states regulate.
- explain how three state services affect you.

52. How State Money Is Spent

Today, states provide many services for people. These services were not needed when our country began.

Why were state services begun? Over the years, each state began providing more and more services for people. The people demanded most of these services. Education became public. Now, everyone has a right to go to school. The states began to fund education.

Utility companies began. These are companies that provide services such as light, power, or water. These companies were regulated. States began to set up police departments. Fire departments were set up. State governments felt a need to help the poor. State services grew as the population of the state grew.

How is the money spent? Most of a state's money is spent on education. Nearly 36% of state money is spent for educational programs. States help fund universities and colleges. Special schools may also get money from states. Public libraries also get money from the state.

What kind of services are included in public welfare? Public welfare programs help needy people. They are for the good or **welfare** of the public. Sometimes, public welfare programs are called social services. Each state sets the rules for its own public welfare programs.

Included in most public welfare or social services programs is help for the elderly. Disabled and handicapped people also receive help. Another part of public welfare is help for those who are out of work.

Public welfare programs give money to needy people. This money helps people buy food and clothes. Some public welfare programs help people find a place to live. These programs are very important.

How does a state protect the health of its people? States spend a lot of money on health services. Health programs are set up for the needy. County nurses visit people who are ill. Public health programs give out medicine. States also set up programs to help people improve their health.

Another service of the state is making sure our food is safe to eat. States also make sure restaurants are clean.

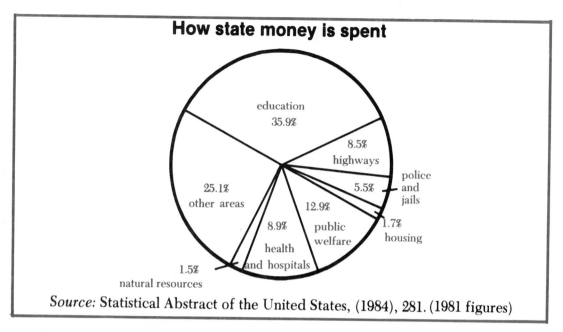

How state money is spent

education
35.9%

8.5%
highways

25.1%
other areas

5.5%

police
and
jails

12.9%

8.9%

public
welfare

1.7%
housing

health
and hospitals

1.5%
natural resources

Source: Statistical Abstract of the United States, (1984), 281. (1981 figures)

How does a state help to protect people's safety? States have many services that help to protect people. State police forces are one example. The state police watch over the whole state. They make sure laws are obeyed on state highways. They help local police forces.

States also have National Guard units. The National Guard helps during times of emergency.

Each state has programs to help prevent crime. Each state also has prisons.

Do states take care of the roads? Yes, states watch over the roads. States make sure the roads are safe. They fix worn roads. Many times federal, state, and local governments work together to build new roads.

Driving laws are decided by each state. States decide how old someone must be to drive. They also decide how heavy trucks can be to travel on state roads.

How do states protect the environment? To keep our environment safe the state and federal governments work together. Businesses are watched so that harm is not done to our air, land, or water.

The states take care of their forest land. Wildlife is closely watched so that it is not harmed. Lakes are kept clean. State parks are set up. Regulations tell how the land may be used. States have much control over how the environment is used.

Are the services the same in each state? States have many of the same services. Some states spend more on some services than on others. It is up to each state to decide how much money to spend. Each state can decide which services are most important.

Look at the pie graph above. It shows how a state spends its money.

53. State Regulation of Business

One of the ways states try to protect their citizens is by regulating business. States regulate both large and small businesses.

What is one way states regulate business? One way states regulate business is by giving out **licenses**. Licenses are permits that allow businesses to perform certain services. Certain standards must be met to get a license.

Licenses are needed by many types of businesses. These include restaurants, beauty shops, auto repair shops, and day care centers.

States also give licenses to different **professions** (jobs). Doctors need a state license. Teachers and nurses need a state license. A license that is good in one state may not be good in another state. It is up to the state to decide which professions need a license. Certain standards must be met for a license.

What is an example of a large business that is regulated? One example of a large business that is regulated is **insurance**. Insurance is a type of protection that people can buy. People buy insurance to protect themselves, their car, or their home.

Many states regulate the insurance business. Insurance rates are watched over. Insurance rules are reviewed. States also license people who sell insurance. In many states, insurance agents must pass a state test to get a license.

Are banks regulated by the state or federal government? Banks are regulated by both state and federal government. Remember that the federal government regulates the flow of money. Many states, though, watch over banks. State government makes sure that banks are fair. Loans and credit practices are watched over, too.

Do states regulate the cost of public utilities? Yes, states regulate public utilities. Utilities include electricity, gas, telephone, and water services. States review utility rates. They watch over the services people receive. States also investigate concerns people have about utility companies.

54. The Cost of State Services

As you can see, states provide many services for people. Protecting the health and welfare of people is an important job. It is also very costly.

What kinds of things do states spend money on? States spend money to provide all of the services you have just read about. This includes money for education and public welfare programs. Money is spent on protecting people's health and supporting hospitals. Money is spent on fixing up the nation's highways. New highways are also built. Money also goes for housing and the rebuilding of cities. This is known as **urban renewal**.

Are the states in debt? Yes, many of the states are in debt. This means that they spend more money than they bring in.

To pay for their expenses, states borrow money. Interest has to be paid on the money borrowed. This interest has become a large item on many state budgets.

Look at the bar graph below. It shows some average state expenses for 1981. Remember these are only *some* state expenses. In 1981, states spent over 485 billion dollars. It is not cheap to run a government!

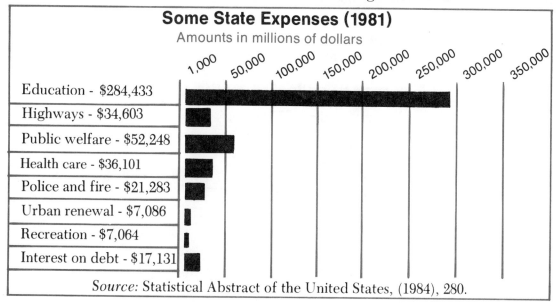

Some State Expenses (1981)

Amounts in millions of dollars

	1,000	50,000	100,000	150,000	200,000	250,000	300,000	350,000
Education - $284,433								
Highways - $34,603								
Public welfare - $52,248								
Health care - $36,101								
Police and fire - $21,283								
Urban renewal - $7,086								
Recreation - $7,064								
Interest on debt - $17,131								

Source: Statistical Abstract of the United States, (1984), 280.

55. Sources of Money

How do states get all their money? Most money comes from taxes.

What kinds of taxes are there? People pay many different kinds of taxes. One kind is sales tax. We pay sales tax on things we buy. Each state has its own type of sales tax.

There are other taxes, too. Income tax is paid on money that is earned. People who earn more usually pay more income tax. People also pay tax on land and buildings they own. **Inheritance** tax is paid on money or property someone receives when some-one dies.

Many states charge a special business tax. This tax is often paid when a business gets a license. Businesses may also pay a special tax called a corporation tax.

Where else do states get money from? States also receive money from the federal government. The federal government may give a state a **grant**. This is money that must be used for a special program.

Some states have **lotteries**. People buy lottery tickets. If their numbers are chosen, they may win a lot of money. Money that is not won is used by the state.

Some states also run state businesses. Money that is earned from these businesses helps pay for state services.

Tax money collected by the states

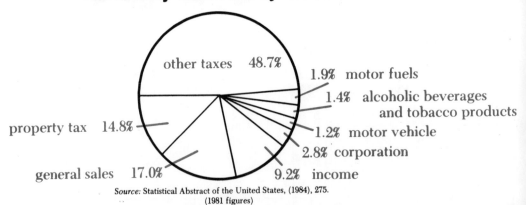

other taxes   48.7%

1.9% motor fuels

1.4% alcoholic beverages
        and tobacco products

property tax   14.8%

1.2% motor vehicle

2.8% corporation

general sales   17.0%

9.2% income

Source: Statistical Abstract of the United States, (1984), 275.
(1981 figures)

Unit 8 Summary

It is the duty of each state to take care of its people. States have services to help people stay safe and healthy. These services are run by the state.

One of a state's largest services is education. State government has much to say on how schools should be run.

Each state also spends money on public welfare. Money for public welfare comes from taxes. It also comes from special funds paid into by people who are employed.

States protect people's safety. State police make sure state laws are obeyed. National Guard units help people during times of great need.

Environmental programs are set up to make sure our water, air, and land are clean. Wildlife is watched over.

Federal, state, and local governments often work together to build state roads. States make sure the roads are safe. States also make the driving rules.

It costs a lot to provide these services. Money for state services comes from many places. Taxes pay for most of the services. States also receive money from the federal government. Some states may get money from lotteries or state owned businesses.

People have come to depend on state services. They help improve many people's lives.

Local Government

STEVE PAQUETTE
FOR ASSEMBLY
119TH DISTRICT
ONON. CAM. SYR.

Local government is really self-government. The people have much say about how local government is run. Local government also works with state and federal governments. Together they make sure people have many services.

Local governments have many duties. One of these duties is record keeping. Local governments may also regulate businesses. They also protect people. This means setting up police and fire departments. It also means having health care centers. Public education is an important part of local government. Schools are under much local control.

How are county governments set up? What kinds of city governments are there? How are townships different from cities? Who are the officials of local government? How does local government affect you? The answers to all these questions are in Unit 9.

By the end of this unit you should be able to:

- explain the duties of five county officials.
- list eight services of local government.
- explain the three kinds of city government.
- explain what a township is.

Sally Rubadeau

56. County Government

<table>
<tr><td colspan="2">Words to know</td></tr>
<tr><td>rural</td><td>zoning</td></tr>
</table>

The word county comes from England. Long ago, England was divided into small areas. Each area was ruled by a count. The area was called a county. The American colonists also divided up the land of each state. They called each smaller area a county.

Why were county governments set up? When our country was first started we did not have such large cities. Most of the land was farmland. Counties were set up to govern the **rural** areas. In many areas of our country, the county is still the only local government. In other areas, the county is made up of almost all cities. Some cities are very large. Chicago, for example, makes up much of Cook County in Illinois. It takes five counties just to make up New York City.

Are all counties the same size? No, the size of counties varies. Some are very large. Some are small. The largest county is San Bernardino County. It is in California. It is 20,102 square miles in size. The smallest county is in New York. It is called New York County. It is only 22 square miles in size.

Each state decides on how many counties it has. Minnesota, for example, has 87 counties. New Hampshire has 10 counties. Texas has 254 counties.

Do county governments have any powers? County government makes sure state services are carried out. County governments have legislative and judicial powers. They also have executive powers. Each county government has powers which cover only its county.

What are the legislative powers of a county? County governments can set taxes. These taxes help to pay for many services. The county government decides how some of the tax money is spent.

Another legislative power of county government is **zoning.** Zoning decides how land may be used. It also helps to decide how land is taxed.

For example, land may be zoned for farmland. Land may also be zoned for business. Or land may be zoned for housing. There are many different ways to zone land. City, village, and town governments can also zone land.

County governments may also set regulations to help protect people's health. These regulations could decide what kinds of businesses there are in the county. They could also decide health standards in public places.

What are the executive powers of a county? Each county is run by a county board or county legislature. The county board or legislature has many departments. The departments cover many areas. These may include roads, hospitals, health care, schools, and social services.

What are the judicial powers of county government? Each county has county judges. Each county also has one or more courts. These courts handle both civil and criminal cases. Some counties have courts to handle family disputes. There are also county courts to settle wills and estates.

Jeffrey J. Strobel

Many counties have special programs to provide balanced meals for the elderly and other low-income people.

57. County Officials

Each county has a county seat. The county seat is a main town or city in the county. All of the county's government is centered in the county seat. Usually, there is a county building. It is here that county officials meet.

Who are the officials of county government? County government has many important officials. These officials are elected by the people of the county. Some of these officials are:

- The county board, or county legislature, governs the county. Members of the county board have both executive and legislative powers.
- The county manager (may also be called county mayor or president) is the chief executive of the county. He or she may be elected or appointed. Not all counties have a county manager.
- The county clerk keeps the county records. Records of births, deaths, and sales of land are kept by the county clerk. Some county clerks watch over elections.
- The recorder of deeds keeps track of land and buildings that are bought and sold. Not all counties have a recorder of deeds. In many counties this work is done by the county clerk.
- The county treasurer takes in the county's money. The county treasurer can also pay the county's bills.
- The county auditor watches over how the money of the county is spent.
- The county assessor decides on how much land and buildings are worth. He **assesses** the value of land and buildings. These values are used to decide how much tax money is paid on the land and buildings.
- The county district attorney represents the county in court.
- The county sheriff makes sure county laws are obeyed. This person watches over the county jail. The county sheriff may also have to sell land and buildings that taxes are not paid on.
- The county coroner investigates deaths that may be part of a crime. The coroner then makes an official report on how the death happened. Not all counties have a county coroner.
- The superintendent of schools watches over educational matters in the county.

58. The Growth of Cities

<table>
<tr><td align="center">Words to know

petition   charter</td></tr>
</table>

Our cities have grown over the years. When our country began there were only a few cities. Most of the people lived on farms. Today there are over 80 cities that have a population of at least 170,000. Some cities are very large. New York is the largest city. Its population is over seven million people. Today most of the people in our country live in cities.

Why have cities grown so large? Our cities have grown because most jobs can be found in the cities. People left the farm to find work in the city. Many people came from other countries. These people looked for jobs in the city. Today our cities support many people.

As cities grew new towns and cities were begun. Large cities now have many towns and cities around them. Some people feel that one day most large cities will be joined together by smaller towns and cities. This has already happened in the eastern part of our country.

How do cities begin? A city begins when a group of people want their area to have its own government. The people write a **petition** to the state. A petition is a written request. It asks for a city **charter**.

What is a city charter? A city charter tells what kind of government the city can have. It is like a constitution for the city. It tells what powers the city government may have. City charters are granted by state legislatures.

59. City Government

There are three kinds of city government. One is called the mayor-council form of government. Another is the council-manager form. The third kind of city government is the commission form.

What is a mayor-council form of government? This is our country's oldest form of city government. It is set up much like a state government. Most cities have a mayor-council form of government.

The mayor is elected by the people of the city. The mayor is the chief executive of the city. The **council** (a group of officials) is also elected.

In some cities the council is elected by the entire city. In other cities, council members are elected by **wards.** A ward is a part of a city. This way council members represent different wards.

The council sets local taxes. Together, the council and mayor make the city's laws. A city law is called an **ordinance.** The mayor makes sure city ordinances are obeyed.

What is the council-manager form of city government? In this plan the council is elected by the people. The council makes the laws for the city. The council hires a manager for the city. The council can also fire the manager. The city manager makes sure the laws of the city are obeyed. Council-manager governments are used in many cities.

What is the commission form of government? In this form the people elect a **commission.** Each member of the commission is called a commissioner. Each commissioner is the head of a department. The commission has executive powers. It also has legislative powers.

Cities with a mayor-council and council-manager form of government may also have city departments. The leaders of the departments may be appointed by the mayor of the council. City departments are very important. They carry out the city's services.

Do city governments provide services for people? Cities provide many services. Education is one of its most important services. Local taxes pay for most of the cost of local schools. Some city governments have much to say on how local schools are run.

Cities provide more than education. They have fire departments, too. They also have police departments to protect people and buildings. Parks are set up by the city. Libraries are also set up.

City services help people. Some people need food. Some need housing. Some need health care. Streets need to be cleaned. Water has to be made pure to drink. Garbage needs to be picked up. Businesses need to be regulated. All this, and more, is taken care of by city government.

Rick Bagley

Being a member of a police department is a hard job. Police are often called upon to help in times of emergency.

60. Towns and Townships

There is another kind of local government. It is called a town. Sometimes, it is called a village. It may also be called a borough. The town may have a mayor or president. The council is called the town board. It may also be called a board of trustees. The town or village officials are elected by the people.

Isn't the town a special form of government in New England? Yes, the town is a special form of government in New England. New England includes the states of Connecticut, Maine, Massachusetts, New Hampshire, Rhode Island, and Vermont. In New England, each county is divided into towns.

How does a New England town government work? Look at the diagram below. It shows how a town government works.

What is a township? A township is another kind of local government. Townships usually govern rural areas. A town board is elected by the people. A township government works very much like the town governments in New England. Within a township there may be a village. A village may have its own government. The village government is usually run by trustees. Some villages also elect a mayor.

How town government works

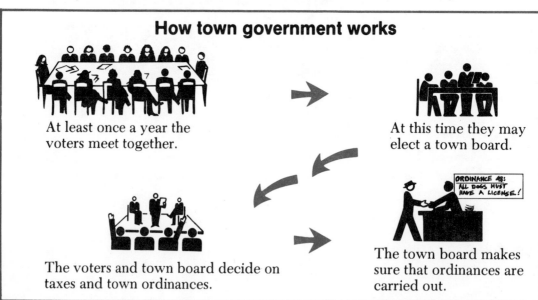

At least once a year the voters meet together.

At this time they may elect a town board.

The voters and town board decide on taxes and town ordinances.

ORDINANCE 48: ALL DOGS MUST HAVE A LICENSE!

The town board makes sure that ordinances are carried out.

Unit 9 Summary

Local governments help make sure state laws are obeyed. They help with federal and state elections. Local governments also make sure state services are carried out. There are many kinds of local government.

One kind of local government is the county. Counties have many powers. They may set taxes. They can zone land. They may set regulations to protect people's health. County officials watch over many county services.

Cities are an important form of local government. Many people live in cities. Cities provide many services.

The town, village, or borough is another kind of local government. A special kind of town government is found in New England. The New England town government is a holdover from when our country first began. It gives people a chance to have a strong say in how government is run.

Local government affects everyone. No matter where you live, some level of local government is working for you. And, at the same time, people have much to say about their local government.

Taxes—A Responsibility

You have been learning about all the services that federal, state, and local governments provide. It is costly to provide these services. And every year it costs more.

Our country has grown a great deal over the years. In 1790, there were almost four million people living in the United States. Today, there are over three million people living just in Chicago, Illinois. The population of the United States is now over 226 million. It costs more and more money to provide services for all these people.

Our country also has other expenses. We are not alone in the world. Money is spent on our defense. We also send money to help foreign countries.

Taxes help to pay for much of this. Taxes have become part of our way of life. They are a responsibility. Americans pay taxes to each level of government—federal, state, and local.

What kinds of taxes are there? How else does the government get money? How is the money spent? What is the national debt? You will find some interesting answers to these questions in Unit 10.

By the end of this unit you should be able to:

- explain how a budget is put together.
- list and explain at least six kinds of taxes.
- explain how three taxes affect you.

61. Direct and Indirect Taxes

There are two kinds of taxes. One is called a direct tax. The other is called an indirect tax. Each kind brings in **revenue** (money) to the government.

What is a direct tax? A direct tax is paid directly to the government. Some examples of a direct tax are:

- Income tax is **levied** (placed) on all forms of income. This includes money received such as salaries and rents. The federal income tax is part of federal law. It was made law in 1913 by the 16th Amendment. Income tax is paid at all levels of government.

- Property tax is paid on property other than land and buildings. Different states have different kinds of property taxes. This tax is paid at the state and local levels.

- Inheritance tax is paid on money or property left to someone after a death. This is a federal and state tax.

- Corporation tax is paid on business earnings. This is another federal and state tax.

- Payroll tax provides money for Social Security. It is listed under FICA (Federal Insurance Contributions Act) on paychecks. This is a federal tax.

What is an indirect tax? An indirect tax is not paid directly to the govern-

1 Control number				
		OMB No. 1545-0008		
2 Employer's name, address, and ZIP code		3 Employer's identification number	4 Employer's State number	
		5 Stat. employee ☐ Deceased ☐ Legal rep. ☐	942 emp. ☐ Subtotal ☐	Void ☐
		6 Allocated tips	7 Advance EIC payment	
8 Employee's social security number	9 Federal income tax withheld	10 Wages, tips, other compensation	11 Social security tax withheld	
12 Employee's name, address, and ZIP code		13 Social security wages	14 Social security tips	
		16 State unemp/dis w/h		
		17 State income tax	18 State wages, tips, etc.	19 Name of State
		20 Local income tax	21 Local wages, tips, etc.	22 Name of locality
Wage and Tax Statement		Copy 1 For State, City, or Local Tax Department Employee's and employer's copy compared. ☐		

Taxes

Federal	State	Local
income	income	real estate
corporation	sales	property
inheritance	inheritance	sales
excise	corporation	excise
customs duties	excise	licenses

ment. It is paid to another taxpayer first. The other taxpayer then passes the tax on to the government. Some indirect taxes are:

- Sales tax is paid on things that are bought. This could include food, clothes, homes, furniture, cars, and other items. Each state decides how much its sales tax will be. The sales tax is a state and local tax.

- Excise tax is paid on the sale of special items. This could include gasoline, guns, tobacco, and alcohol. Excise tax can be paid to all levels of government.

As you can see, tax money comes from many sources. Look at the chart above. It shows the taxes paid to the different levels of government.

An excise tax is paid on tobacco products such as cigarettes.

62. Other Sources of Government Money

The government gets much of its revenue from taxes. But there are other ways for the government to get money, too. The federal government can do any of the following to raise more money:

- It can print more money.
- It can put more money into circulation.
- It can borrow money.
- It can increase taxes.
- It can cut costs.

How can the government print more money? The Constitution of the United States gives Congress the power to make money. Congress has given this power to the executive branch. Now, the Treasury Department has the power to print money.

But printing more money is not always a good idea. Everytime extra money is printed, the value of all money goes down. This is why the making of **counterfeit** (fake) money is such a serious crime.

Who decides on the country's money flow? The Federal Reserve Board regulates the flow of money. It decides if more money should be printed. It also decides how much credit banks should give. The Federal Reserve Board is an independent agency. It decides on the money flow in the country. Congress cannot tell the Federal Reserve Board what to do. The president cannot tell the Federal Reserve Board what to do either.

Does the federal government ever borrow money? Yes, the federal government borrows money. It has to do this because it spends more money than it takes in. This means that the federal government is in **debt**. Look at the graph on the next page. It shows how our country's debt is growing.

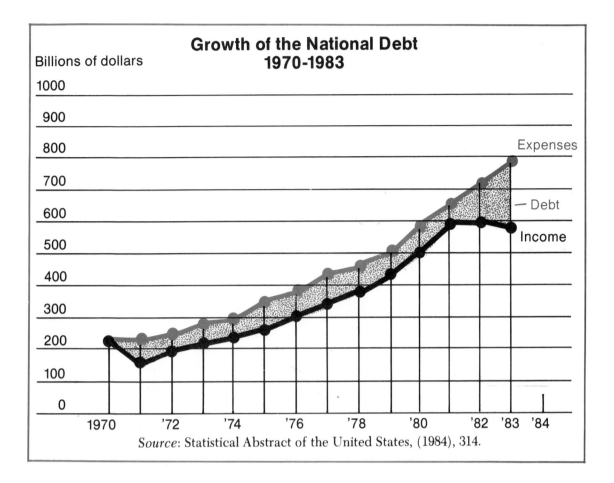

Growth of the National Debt 1970-1983

Billions of dollars

Expenses

— Debt

Income

1970 '72 '74 '76 '78 '80 '82 '83 '84

Source: Statistical Abstract of the United States, (1984), 314.

The federal government is not the only one to borrow money. State and local governments borrow money, too.

How does the government borrow money? The government borrows from persons, banks, and large businesses. The government sells bonds. It pays **interest** to the people who buy bonds. Interest is the extra money paid for being able to borrow money.

Perhaps you have a United States Savings Bond. If so, when you bought the bond, you were loaning the government money. When you cash the bond in, the government has to pay you what you paid for the bond plus a small amount more. This is how interest works.

Why doesn't the government just cut costs? Our government has many services. People have grown used to having these services. It is hard for the government to cut back on them.

There is also **inflation** to consider. Inflation is when the overall cost of things goes up. During times of inflation, the price of services goes up. The government often must spend more money for the same services than it used to.

63. How Government Money Is Spent

Federal, state, and local governments make budgets. A budget tells how the government plans to spend its money. The executive branch puts the budget together. The legislative branch approves the budget.

How are budgets put together? Each department decides how much revenue it will need. It checks to see how much its services will cost. The department head gives this information to the head of the executive branch.

The cost of each service is looked over. Some services are given more money. Some services are given less money. Some services are added. Some are dropped. Money for each department is agreed on. A total amount of money to run the government is decided on. The head of the executive branch passes the budget to the legislative branch.

The federal government has grown. How has its budget changed over the years? During the last 100 years, the federal government has increased its services. These services cost money. The federal budget has had to grow. The bar graph below shows how the federal budget has changed.

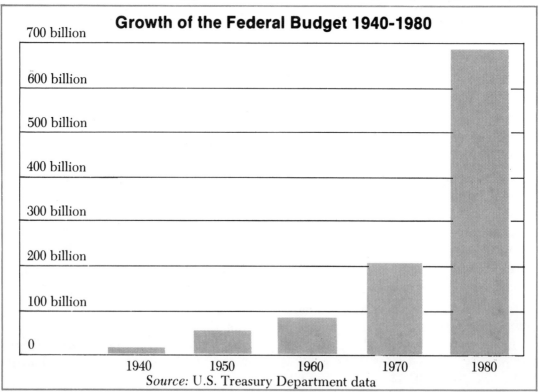

Growth of the Federal Budget 1940-1980

Source: U.S. Treasury Department data

Unit 10 Summary

Every government needs revenue to work. Government is set up to help people. People pay for government.

The cost of government has grown over the years. It is not fun to pay for these costs. But paying taxes is a citizen's duty.

Taxes pay for many of the government's bills. Taxes are paid to federal, state, and local governments. there are many kinds of taxes. Income taxes bring in the most money to government. Payroll taxes also bring in much money.

The United States spends more money than it takes in. It must get more money to cover its costs. One way it gets money is by borrowing. Another way is to increase taxes. The federal government can also put more money into circulation.

Every level of government puts together a budget. The budget shows how much money is to be spent. Budgets get larger every year as costs increase and people want more services.

Being a Citizen

America is sometimes called a "melting pot." This is because people have come to the United States from all over the world.

Many people still come to America. They come hoping for a better life. They want to become citizens. But, what does being a good citizen mean?

Good citizens take an active part in local government. They speak out. They help to improve local government. Good citizens also learn about what is happening in their state. They also know what is happening in the country.

Good citizens keep in touch with their elected officials. They let them know how they feel about what government is doing. A good citizen also remembers to vote.

What rights do you have as a citizen? How do people become citizens? How can you take an active part in improving your city or town? How important is voting? Unit 11 will help you find the answers to these and other questions.

By the end of this unit you should be able to:

- explain how someone becomes a citizen.
- know a citizen's rights.
- explain the Voting Rights Act of 1965.
- list three ways you can become a part of local government.

Ron Byers

64. Becoming a Citizen

People who come to our country to live are called immigrants. Not everyone who wants to is allowed to move to the United States. A person who wants to live in our country must first get a **visa.** A visa is a document that allows a non-citizen to stay in the country. Visas are granted by the Department of Justice.

Does a visa grant citizenship to an immigrant? No, a visa does not grant citizenship. A visa just allows the person to stay in the United States for a certain time.

What rights do immigrants have? Immigrants have many rights in the United States. They may buy and sell property. They may use government services. They pay taxes. An immigrant may become a United States citizen.

Are there any rights immigrants do not have? Immigrants may only vote if they become citizens. Also, immigrants must let the government know where they live every year. An immigrant can be sent back to the country he or she came from. This could happen if the immigrant broke a federal law.

How many people immigrate to the United States every year? Many people come to live in the United States. During the 1970's an average of 396 thousand people immigrated each year. Since 1820, 49 million people have immigrated to the United States. These people have come from countries all over the world.

How does an immigrant become a citizen? Immigrants who would like to become citizens must ask the Immigration and Naturalization Service. An immigrant who becomes a citizen is called a **naturalized** citizen.

Who can become a citizen of the U.S.? An immigrant must meet certain standards to be granted citizenship. To become a United States citizen the immigrant must:

- be at least 18 years old.
- have lived in the United States for the last five years.
- be able to show a good use of the English language.
- show an understanding of the government.
- be a lawful person.
- have two people who will speak in favor of him.

Who grants citizenship to an immigrant? Every immigrant wishing to become a citizen must have a hearing.

The hearing is a meeting between the immigrant and an official of the Immigration and Naturalization Service. The official asks the immigrant many questions. The official then tells a judge about the hearing. The judge decides if the immigrant should be granted citizenship. The judge then either gives or does not give citizenship to the immigrant.

What are the rights of a naturalized citizen? A naturalized citizen has all the same rights as a person born in the United States. All naturalized citizens take an oath. The oath says that the naturalized citizen will obey the law. It also says that the naturalized citizen will defend the country.

Our country is a nation of immigrants. We can share and learn about different ways of life from each other. This helps make America unique.

65. Voting

All United States citizens may vote. People must **register** to vote. To register, you fill out a small form. Then your name is added to a list of voters. To vote, a person must be at least 18 years old. In most states, people used to have to be 21 to vote. The voting age was lowered to 18 by the 26th Amendment. This happened in 1971.

State laws may keep some people from voting. In some states people convicted of bad crimes may not vote. Each state also says that a citizen must have lived in the state for so many days before being able to vote.

The poll tax kept many people from voting. What was the poll tax? Before 1964, some states had a poll tax. (A **poll** is the place where you vote.) Anyone who wanted to vote had to pay the poll tax. The poll tax kept many poor people from voting. They did not have money to pay a tax to vote. In 1964, the 24th Amendment was passed. It says that states may not charge a poll tax to vote in federal elections. In 1966, the Supreme Court said that states also could not charge a poll tax to vote in state elections.

Besides the 24th Amendment, are there any other amendments that give rights to voters? Yes, four other amendments to the Constitution grant voters certain rights. These four are the 15th, 19th, 23rd, and 26th Amendments.

The 15th Amendment was passed in 1870. It passed after the Civil War. It gave people who had been slaves the right to vote. The 15th Amendment says that people cannot be kept from voting because of their race or color.

The 19th Amendment was passed in 1920. It gives women the right to vote. It says that no person shall be denied the right to vote because of the person's sex.

The 23rd Amendment was passed in 1961. It says that the District of Columbia may have electors for electing the president and vice-president. It is the capital of our country. It is where our federal government is centered.

The 26th Amendment was passed in 1971. It says that all citizens 18 years of age and older may vote.

What is the Voting Rights Act? The Voting Rights Act was passed in 1965. It made it a federal crime to try to keep someone from voting. It says that the federal government can take over voter registration if any of three things happen.

- Some people who are able to vote are not allowed to vote.
- People are asked to take a test showing they know how to read.
- Only half of the voters that can vote have registered to vote.

Have there been any changes to the Voting Rights Act? In 1975 amendments to the act were added to help non-English speaking people to vote. The amendments say that registration and voting must be in two languages. The amendments are for areas where at least 5% of the population are non-English speaking. For example, all of Texas must allow voting in both English and Spanish. Parts of the western states must allow voting in English and Native American. Parts of California must allow voting in English, Spanish, and Chinese.

Fritz Photography

Before you can vote, you must register. Registering to vote is easy.

66. The Importance of Voting

Voting is very important. Voting elects officials who make laws for you. Every citizen's vote counts. In small towns an election can be won by one or two votes. Even in large cities it is important that every citizen votes.

What is an example of a close election when everyone's vote counted? The 1983 election held in Chicago, Illinois is a good example of how important everyone's vote is. Chicago is the third largest city in our country. In 1983, Harold Washington was elected mayor of Chicago. Mr. Washington is Chicago's first black mayor. He was elected by 51% of the vote. This was a very close election. Everyone's vote was very important.

Do most people who can vote do so? Sadly, many people who can vote do not. Voter turn-out is usually low for primary elections. Many people do not vote even to elect the president of the United States. In 1972, only 55.5% of those in the country who could vote did. During the 1976 election for president only 54% of those able to vote did. In the 1980 election, again, only 54% voted. It is important for more people to vote. Every vote does count.

UPI/Bettmann Archive

Rev. Jesse Jackson leads a rally in Los Angeles. Jackson, a 1984 presidential candidate, was very active in getting black and other minority groups to register and vote.

67. Becoming Involved

Just how do people become a part of their government? Voting is one very important way. Following the news every day is also good to do. Another way is to be active in your **community**. Your community is the area you live in.

How can a person be active in his community? One important way is to go to city or town meetings. Learn about new laws that are being talked over. Let your local officials know how you feel about what is happening in your community.

School board meetings are also important to go to. Learn about new plans for your school. Give ideas to try to improve your school.

How can people get in touch with their representatives? There are many ways people can get in touch with their representatives. One way is to write letters. Find out who your elected officials are. Write to them about laws you support. You should also let them know when you are against a law.

Many times elected representatives hold meetings. The public is asked to come to the meetings. This is a good time to talk to your representatives.

Jim Tyson

There are many opportunities to become involved in local government. School board meetings are a good chance to hear the opinions of people in the community.

The use of a petition is also a good way to show your feelings. Many times there are a lot of people who like or dislike a law. These people may sign a petition. The petition tells their representatives how they feel about an issue. Petitions can be used to change some laws. New laws can also be brought about by petitions.

Is support of elected officials important? Yes, support is very important. Help people you would like to see in office get elected. Work to re-elect officials you feel are doing a good job. You might also try running for office yourself someday.

How else can you help your community? Offering to help in community events is a good way to help your community. Give your free time to others. This could be getting together a clean-up drive. It could be helping out at a day-care center. It could mean working with older people. There are many ways to help improve your community.

Arnold J. Saxe

New York City Mayor Ed Koch and Al Del Bello campaign in the 1982 democratic primary for governor and lieutenant governor.

Unit 11 Summary

Our country is a free country. People have come from all over the world to live in America. Many people from other countries have become American citizens. A naturalized citizen has the same rights as an American born citizen.

Voting is an important right. We elect people to make laws for us. Today, many people do not vote. More people should vote. Voting is one way we tell our representatives how we feel about laws that have been made.

People should be a part of their government. One way to do this is by voting. Another way is by helping in your community. People can help others get elected. A person may also choose to run for office.

The writers of the Constitution wanted government to be for the people. For this to happen people must take an active part in their government. Government works for people when people work to improve their government.

Index